REFORMATION OLD AND NEW

REFORMATION OLD AND NEW

(A Tribute to Karl Barth)

Edited by

F. W. CAMFIELD, M.A., D.D.

(Vicar of Churchstow with Kingsbridge, Devon)

LUTTERWORTH PRESS
LONDON and REDHILL

THIS BOOK IS PRODUCED IN
COMPLETE CONFORMITY WITH THE
AUTHORIZED ECONOMY STANDARDS

Printed in Great Britain by
The Camelot Press Ltd., London and Southampton

CONTENTS

FOREWORD

THIS book is intended as a tribute of gratitude and regard to Professor Karl Barth, and as a greeting to him on the attainment of his sixtieth birthday. Its contributors are drawn from different sections of the Christian Church and they represent various tendencies in British theological thought. They would not wish therefore to call themselves "Barthians", an appellation which Barth himself repudiates. But they are all conscious of having received from his theological teaching stimulation and enrichment, and they feel that a wider knowledge of that teaching cannot but contribute to the clarification of the mind of the Church as it seeks to relate the everlasting gospel to the circumstances and needs of a rapidly changing world. They hope and pray that health and length of days may be given to Professor Barth so that he may complete the Dogmatic work to which he has put his hand, and which is now in mid-career. They would further put on record their sense of the high value of his testimony to the authority and sovereignty of the Word of God in the struggle against pagan and idolatrous ideologies; and they would offer grateful recognition of the part which his influence played during the recent war, in illumining the mind and confirming the purpose of Christian people in many lands in opposition to the evil will of National Socialist totalitarianism.

But this book has not been written merely in honour of a man. Its title is *Reformation Old and New,* and this title designates its purpose. All its contributors believe in the Holy Catholic Church, and they see in its life and witness the divinely-appointed agency for the reformation and redemption of human life and society. They believe that the Church has been called into being and is sustained in its life by the Word and Spirit of God, and that it can serve the world only as, by ever renewed endeavour, it seeks to place itself under the control of that Word and Spirit. Such an endeavour must always mean reformation of a very radical kind. They would interpret the work of Karl Barth as, above all, a prayer for this reformation and renewal; and, whatever may be their agreements or

7

disagreements with his theological views, they would associate themselves with this prayer. This is the spirit in which they have written, and in which they seek to be understood.

It only remains for the editor to acknowledge with gratitude the warm and friendly co-operation of his fellow contributors, and the encouragement and support of the Lutterworth Press.

F. W. CAMFIELD.

KINGSBRIDGE VICARAGE,
May, 1946.

ABBREVIATED REFERENCES

In footnote references to Barth's *Die Kirchliche Dogmatik*, the following abbreviations are used for convenience:

Dog., I, 1,=*Die Lehre vom Wort Gottes. Prolegomena zur Kirchlichen Dogmatik, Erster Halbband*, Chr. Kaiser Verlag, München, 1932.

Dog., I, 2, = *Die Lehre vom Wort Gottes. Prolegomena zur Kirchlicheu Dogmatik, Zweiter Halbband*, Verlag der evangelischen Buchhandlung Zollikon, 1938.

Dog., II, 1,=*Die Lehre von Gott, Erster Halbband*, Verlag der evangelischen Buchhandlung Zollikon, 1940.

Dog., II, 2,=*Die Lehre von Gott, Zweiter Halbband*, Evangelischer Verlag A. G. Zollikon, Zürich, 1942.

Part One

DEVELOPMENT AND PRESENT STAGE OF THE THEOLOGY OF KARL BARTH

by

THE EDITOR

CHAPTER I

THE THEOLOGY OF KARL BARTH AS A SPIRITUAL MOVEMENT

THAT in Karl Barth a religious portent of arresting significance had appeared was perceived even in the English world, which has the reputation of being somewhat slow to recognize such things, at a comparatively early date. Certainly at first, the disposition was common to regard it as a quite ephemeral phenomenon, boding no more than a symptom of that irrational revolt which, in the years following the War of 1914-18, swept over well-nigh the whole of European life both outwardly and inwardly. Civilization was a failure. Liberalism was bankrupt. Progress was an illusion. How could theology hope to escape from the universal shaking? Since everywhere the presuppositions which had supported the ordered development of life and thought in the long peace before the war were being sharply and even savagely questioned, how could it happen otherwise than that theology should experience scars? A tottering world could scarcely be without its angry prophets. Were they not therefore to be expected within the sphere of the Church? But the forces of equilibrium would soon assert themselves, and the wild cries of men in revolt would be lost in the winds of the passing storm.

It was in some such fashion that men, for the most part, thought and felt at first when Barth appeared with his *Commentary on the Epistle to the Romans*, which "fell like a bomb on the playground of the theologians".[1] He was a post-war phenomenon and would soon have his day and cease to be.

Nevertheless, the theological world was not entirely at its ease as Barth's voice fell upon its ears. It had long felt, dimly or clearly, that all was not well with it. Since it could not but be aware at the back of its mind that its concern was with a very real, positive, and commanding word and revelation coming straight from God Himself; since it knew deep down in its heart that it

[1] Karl Adam, quoted in *The Significance of Karl Barth*, by McConnachie, p. 43

had to deal with a gospel and not merely with an optimistic world-view; since it could not entirely escape the conviction that a theologian was called to be something more and something other than a philosopher, or an historian, or a psychologist, with a spiritual outlook and spiritual intuitions; it was, sub-consciously at any rate, ready to be questioned about the course which for decades it had, in the main, been pursuing. It had been so apologetic, and so accommodating in its relations to what had been extolled as modern thought, but which the catastrophe of the war had so rudely shaken. It had felt itself answerable to the discoveries, and not to the discoveries alone, but to the whole world-view of modern science, both physical and psychological, of philosophy, and of culture generally. It had shown a somewhat nervous eagerness to dovetail the truths for which the Bible stood sponsor into a general interpretation of life built up from the more spiritual aspects of modern life and thought, to represent theology as the ripe fruit growing on the tree of a general philosophy of religion, and to crown and complete the spiritual evolution of man with the figure of Jesus Christ. And somehow this did not seem to fit in with the fundamental outlook of the New Testament, with its redemptive, supernatural, and eschatological emphases.

Nevertheless, theology had felt it its duty to justify itself before the world of science and philosophy. How otherwise could it prevent itself from being isolated within the field of humanistic culture and thus from being forced into surrender? So it had been looking round in this field and trying to help itself to whatever it could find there which would preserve its life and enable it to make a show. But of late it had become somewhat disquieted over this policy which it had been pursuing. It found itself in danger of being secularized. It had found itself confronted with the question as to whether it was, as a distinct and separate science, necessary at all. Could not theology after all be subsumed under a general philosophy of religion in which the distinctive Christian gospel would be reduced to a position of only relative significance and validity? And in that form must it not content itself with a struggle against the New Psychology, which, like all the struggles against the advancing tides of secular science, seemed to be a losing one?

14

So, presently, men began to give rather more serious attention to this new prophet, Karl Barth. He could, of course, have little that was positive to contribute, but he might have a very definite negative value. He might be useful in that he was calling a halt to that secularizing of thought which was going on in the Church, to the *Anschluss* of theology with history, psychology, philosophy, and humanism. It might even be conceded that he possessed some positive value in re-orientating theology, in calling it back to the Bible and to the revelation for which the Bible stood sponsor, in suggesting that revelation possessed its own norms which were, after all, different from those of secular science, in making it clear that the kingdom of God was something other than human evolution and progress, and that one did not talk of God by "talking of man in a loud voice".

Thus Barth came to be looked upon as in some sense a prophet, a rather noisy and one-sided prophet, but still a voice to which one should not be entirely deaf. One might stop for a moment to listen to him; for then one could proceed with theological work with a somewhat better conscience.

At first Barth seemed to claim little more than this from the theological world. He was, it is true, somewhat restive in being hailed as a prophet. There were many prophets in the land, many who were all too ready to deliver their souls, and who were having rather a good time in the post-war world by passing judgment on the whole range of what had been taken as culture and civilization. Barth did not want to add to their number, and he was rather mortified than otherwise in that he was becoming a "best-seller". But he was not quite sure that he wanted to be a theologian. Did he not want most of all to be a preacher, to proclaim the Word of God to men in all the mystery of their life? He had stood Sunday by Sunday in the pulpit faced by people who had come to Church presumably because they expected to hear something which they could hear nowhere else; and it had been borne across his mind and heart that the office of the preacher was not to be a "commentator on infinity", not to give expression to human insights and aspirations with reference to the spiritual, but to announce a message from God. How could one do that? How was preaching possible when one perceived what it signified? He was amazed to discover that the tasks and problems of the preacher seemed to be regarded in such a leisurely fashion by the theologian.[1] It would appear as if the utterances of the preacher were to be valued simply, or at any rate chiefly, for their inspirational power, while the content of the Christian revelation was to be left to the academic theologian. Barth felt that in this way the theologian was claiming for himself both too much and too little; too much, in that the great truths of revelation could not be put at the disposal of the man who was largely withdrawn from the direct responsibility of proclamation; and too little, in that the theologian held a certain authoritative position with regard to the continuous witness of the Church. The theologian must be both the servant of the preacher and his critic and judge. In fact, theology existed in order that there might be true preaching, in order that the Word of God might be proclaimed to men with authority and power. Barth rather shrank from being a theologian himself, but, being a preacher, he could not leave theology alone. So, outwardly at any rate, he largely fell in at first with the general estimate of him as a sign or portent that things were not well in the theological world, that the theologians in their relative detachment from the preacher's activity of proclamation were mumbling about God rather than speaking of Him; that they were in the way of forgetting that their business was to do something more and something other than dish up in a spiritual form the kind of thing that workers in other fields were dishing up in a secular form. Borrowing a phrase of Kierkegaard he compared himself to a "pinch of spice" in the theologians' meal.

He soon discovered, however, that in that regard he was being fairly generally digested. His protest obtained a hearing and some measure of approval, so that men came soon to feel that they had done with him. He was slipping into a figure of the past, and though, so far as he personally was concerned, that mattered not at all, it became all too clear to him that a mere protest and even a sharp and challenging call were insufficient to arrest the tide of secularization in theology. Men went on their way with all the better heart because they had

[1] See *The Word of God and the Word of Man*, Eng. trans., pp. 100-102

16

stopped a moment to listen to him, and, as a result, were disposed to make changes of emphasis here and there. The leopard, he felt, was changing his spots, but not his skin. The theologians were still playing the old game. They were still hankering after a synthesis between revelation and "reason", were still striving to bring revelation into line with modern thought instead of bringing modern thought into line with revelation. In fact, their strategy was not changed, only their tactics.

There was another feature in the situation which was equally serious. Barth found himself in the position of a prophet who was forming a school. "Barthians" began to appear, and many of these filled him with dismay. There were those who seemed to regard Barth's own speech and mannerisms, his "vagaries" as he called them, as if they were his essential message. His epigrams, violent antitheses, audacious paradoxes, were to be the new language of theology. What vapourings there were with such words as "death-line", empty space", "crisis", "the wholly other", and so on! How splendid to think that one could, as it were, cry up God by crying down man! Barth became appalled at the negative nature that was being attributed to his message. And even where a more modest and sober temper prevailed, there was the tendency to suppose that the promised land of Christian truth and understanding was now close at hand, and that the desperate confusion of the Church could be remedied by the calm taking over of a new set of theological watchwords.

Barth saw that he must completely divest himself of the prophet's mantle and set to work in an ordered and thorough-going fashion in the theological field. He was driven into theology on the big scale almost against his will. He was a theologian with the manner of a preacher who speaks because he cannot remain silent, because constraint is laid upon him which he dare not resist. He had learned out of the Scriptures that God had given to man a sure ground of trust in His Word in Jesus Christ, and that therefore man must not put his trust in anything but that Word; that any movement to the right or left of this straight and narrow way was a movement into the void. What could theology be, if it were to remain true to its nature, but a thorough-going articulation and expression of the witness borne in Scripture to that Word? Was man to be exhorted from the pulpit to put his trust in that and in that alone, and then directly he left the Church and entered the realms of science, philosophy, and culture, to be invited to find other grounds of trust in these regions? Was it to be suggested to him by the very theology which was concerned with this Word that his trust in it needed support and confirmation from other sources, as if the Word itself were not self-authenticating and self-sufficient? Was it even to be suggested to him that his trust in the Word of God could only be the confirmation of a trust arising from other sources? And was the sole-sufficiency of Jesus Christ, in other words His Lordship, merely a principle of piety which could operate only in a loose and weakened form when piety must give place to the demands of strict and accurate thought and investigation? Barth saw that the issue could no longer be deferred. A new Dogmatics was needed to meet the situation, new not in the modernistic sense, for what were modernistic theologies but rehashes of old heresies, but new in the sense that it must be utterly and exclusively a theology of the Word of God, a theology of revelation, a theology which learned its content, its methods, and its very forms of language from revelation itself.

The new Dogmatics seemed at first to be a quite manageable undertaking. Inasmuch as its governing principle precluded anything in the nature of the old apologetic, any attempt to justify theology before the bar of the natural reason, the task which Barth set himself seemed measurably straightforward. An introductory volume setting forth the preliminaries, or prolegomena, would seem to be necessary in order to make quite clear the aim and purpose of the whole work. But this introductory volume must simply be a kind of prospectus of the ground to be covered. Barth was convinced that one had not to do a lot of other things before theology proper could be ventured upon. One could and must begin at once with the subject-matter of theology itself. For example, it was not necessary and it was not justifiable to expend time and effort in proving that there was a God and that He had given a revelation of Himself. What was essential in this regard would appear *a posteriori*, and in the course of the theological exposition itself. If God had spoken, since He had spoken, the question of His existence and the problems bound up with it would receive clarification in the investigation of what He had said. Whether He had, in fact, given a revelation of Himself, and what that revelation was, would become evident as the Church was taken seriously in its claim to be the mouthpiece of the Word of God. Theology had simply to be itself. It had not to spend time and energy in claiming the right to exist. It had simply to march forward.

So Barth embarked upon a kind of five years' plan. He had but to arrange and expand the material which he had been accumulating, and issue it in volume after volume in quick succession. But matters turned out very differently from what he had expected. His first volume encountered so heavy a fire of criticism from colleagues that he became convinced that he had been travelling too quickly. He could not blind himself to the fact that much of this criticism was justified. He had not sufficiently clarified his ideas. And he had even given rise to the very suspicion which he was anxious to avoid, that in the very effort to disentangle himself from philosophical presuppositions he had in some sense fallen victim to them. Had he not, for example, in his insistence on the Word of God as event in the world into which man's existence is inevitably drawn, gone some way in involving himself in that Existentialism which marked the latest phase in German philosophical thinking? Had he not made the man who is gripped by the Word of God, to some extent, at any rate, the subject of his investigation and a factor in revelation itself? Had he not been at least on the way towards evolving an anthropology as a basis for his theology? Certainly he had not intended to do this. He had intended to move in a dimension altogether different from that of the philosophers. But had he altogether succeeded in doing this? He was convinced that it was necessary for him to go over the whole ground again, and much more carefully. A huge mountain of confusion and misunderstanding must be moved out of the way before the march forward could properly begin.

Moreover, he was becoming increasingly uneasy with regard

to some of those who were commonly looked upon as his allies in the campaign which he was waging. Were their objectives sufficiently one with his own? Gogarten, for example, was insisting that, since the Word of God was addressed to man, and since man was involved in history, theology could not be pursued in independence of the historical actuality of the man who was called upon to take account of it. There could not be "a timeless theology", a theology which ignored the special nature of the times in which it was being written, a theology which aimed at being the same for every age and stage in the process of historical unfolding. He was protesting that Barth was in danger of isolating God and God's Word from man's history and man's life. Though disclaiming any desire after a natural theology, Gogarten was insisting that the laws of God were deeply embedded in the structure of the created order, and specially in the order of man's life and history. It was not that these laws were discoverable apart from a special act of divine revelation, but that this special revelation could not be properly understood in independence of a general investigation of man's historical nature.[1] What that meant was presently to be made clear when in the early days of the National Socialist movement in Germany, Gogarten declared that the law of God for Germany was given in the *nomos* or special character of the German soul. Barth felt that the whole purpose of his work was being imperilled by Gogarten's contentions. He could see in them nothing more than a recrudescence of natural theology in another form, a form even more deadly than the old, because it wore the garb of revelation and offered itself as a means of actualizing divine reality within the temporal and historical order. In any case, it was all too evident to him that Gogarten's intentions were not the same as his own. Gogarten was just as concerned as the old liberal Protestants had been to deliver theology from its isolation, and that concern was proving to be the main motive of his theological work. Barth was not to be influenced by this concern. He felt that any concern beyond the one concern that theology should be true to the Word of God as witnessed to in the Scriptures meant inevitably its secularization. And one

[1] See *Gericht oder Skepsis*, a criticism of Barth's theology in general

may be permitted to point out that Gogarten's appeal to history has been very effectually answered by history itself. The secularizing and paganizing of the German Church by the so-called German Christian movement, over which Gogarten cast the aegis of his theology, became a deadly fact.

With another hitherto close colleague, Emil Brunner, Barth began to feel himself increasingly at variance.[1] Brunner also was troubled about the isolation of theology, but he sought to break it down in a somewhat different way from that of Gogarten. He felt that the great hindrance to the acceptance of revelation was man's confidence in his independent and autonomous reason. This confidence must be broken down, for it was a false confidence. It made man his own centre and excluded the recognition of all reality which did not fall within the subject-object relation. This independence and autonomy of the natural reason was in Brunner's view the root and source of all sin and the perversion of all true understanding. Before Dogmatics could properly begin, there was need of what Brunner called Eristics, that is, a philosophical disputation which would prepare man's mind for the reception of revelation by smashing the axiom of the independent and autonomous reason. Such a disputation would have, in addition, to demonstrate the existence of a point of contact in man's nature, and apart from the action of revelation, to which revelation might link itself; for without the exhibition of such a point of contact the axiom of the autonomous reason could not be overthrown. If man's reason was, in fact, not autonomous, then, argued Brunner, it must be in some sense open to a reality transcending the subject-object relation, open in fact to revelation. Brunner was, therefore, prepared to give a small and strictly limited place to natural theology. The fact was, he was very anxious to commend Christianity to the intellectuals, and he felt that he could not get at them until he had met them on their own ground and overthrown their fundamental presupposition. Barth, though comprehending and in some measure sharing his concern, was apprehensive of the way in which Brunner was seeking to meet it. In any case, whether this Eristics was justified or not, it could have no place in the

[1] See *Natur und Gnade*, and Barth's *Nein*

sphere of theology. Revelation could not speak to man on his own ground. It must be trusted to set up its own point of contact with man's nature and man's mind. It could not permit natural theology of any kind to share in the work which a theology of revelation alone could accomplish.

Accordingly, Barth felt that he must begin all over again with his Dogmatic work. He must not aim at quick results, and his five years' plan must go by the board. And he must not, directly at any rate, look for allies in the work of theological renewal, for those whom he had regarded as such had aims and purposes which were not his. His mind was now clear as to what he was about, and in two volumes of vast bulk in which every statement was made with careful precision and guarded against misunderstandings and objections, the *Prolegomena*, dealing with the Biblical conception of the Word of God, and introducing the fundamental doctrines of revelation which were to form the subjects of later detailed investigations, were laid down.

Scarcely was the first of these two volumes out when there occurred the great upheaval of the National Socialist revolution. Barth felt that the line which he was taking was being amply vindicated. For what was happening within the German Church? As if, he says, by a veritable psychosis, teachers, leaders, pastors, and students, were acclaiming Hitler as a kind of new Messiah, and the new German national consciousness as a new revelation of the Spirit of God.[1] Gogarten went over to the German Christians. Even Brunner was regarded by them with a measure of approval, as affording them grist to their mill with his natural theology. Was it not now crystal clear that any theology which looked to sources of revelation outside of God's Word in Jesus Christ was a servant of the false gods? And when the dragooning of the Church by the Government began, Barth discovered that the one way of offering any effective resistance was to hold fast to the one ground of Christian security, the Word of God in Jesus Christ attested by the Scriptures. There has rarely been in the whole history of the Church a theologian so amply vindicated by history as Karl Barth. That man's trust must be in God alone; that God can be known only as He reveals Himself; that His

---

[1] See *Theological Existence To-day*, Eng. trans., pp. 55-56

revelation of Himself is nothing but Himself in revelation; that nothing in man's nature, man's life, man's history, man's world, can be, simply as such, a constituent in revelation; that there must be no question of integrating revelation into man's knowledge and experience of the world but that this knowledge and experience must be integrated into revelation, and into revelation by revelation itself—all this began to sound, not as whirling words of irrational paradox, but as words of truth and soberness. But are we putting the matter aright? Are we simply flinging out a challenge which might all too easily be taken up and thrown back? We are certainly doing this if we are laying the emphasis on the negatives; if our purpose is primarily the denial of the competence of man's reason and the validity of his experience. Barth, however, will not have us do this. He will have us follow the positive way of revelation itself; confine ourselves to the way of God to man as it stands in the witness of the Scriptures to Jesus Christ; take our bearings from that movement which is not a movement *of* the world, but a movement *to* the world, and draw all our insights and understandings concerning the relation of God to the world and of the world to God from thence; thus, not argue about natural theology and set out to refute it, but turn our backs upon it and take another way; not discuss the point of contact between revelation and the natural reason, but perceive the connection which revelation itself establishes with reason; not labour after an interpretation of man as an historical being, but discern how revelation makes him a truly historical being. He will have us free our mind from all anxieties about ourselves and our rights, and make our thinking an act of pure obedience, in the confidence that, in our obedience, we shall find the rightful demands of our reason met and satisfied.

The integrity of this theological purpose became more and more evident as the Church struggle in Germany proceeded. In the early stages of the Revolution, Barth contented himself with simply continuing his work as theological thinker and teacher. This was not only the wisest and safest way to act, it was in his opinion the only true way. Let it be established that the Church was responsible for her message to the Word of God alone, and she would prove a firm bulwark against any totalitarian idolatry and an effective champion of soul freedom. Unfortunately, however, the Church's leaders seemed to have fallen asleep at their posts. They were permitting their theological existence to be filched from them. Barth came to see that the situation called for more than theological work in the narrower sense of that term. The theologian must become also prophet, and even, in a sense, ecclesiastical statesman. Truly, he shrank from both offices, so far as he himself was concerned. Yet he could not ignore the fact that prophet and ecclesiastical statesman both had their proper place within the Church. Accordingly, while still remaining theologian *par excellence*, he lifted up the prophet's voice; and his tract, *Theological Existence To-day*, relentlessly tore away every illusion which might conceal the real issue. To every claim that the new spirit of German nationalism was to be regarded as a movement of the Spirit of God to which independent revelationary significance belonged; to every suggestion that it was to be interpreted as a point of connection between the Word of God and the un- folding of human history; to every demand that at this point Church and world should meet, Barth's mighty "No" rever- berated round the Christian world. Moreover, the Christian statesman must appear on the field. The Church must stand before the world clearly and unambiguously erecting the standard of her confession. Accordingly, at Barmen, the foundation of the Confessional Church of Germany was firmly laid, and an explicit repudiation of every authority for faith save the one authority of the Word of God revealed in Jesus Christ and witnessed to by the Scriptures was made. Barth was surely not wrong in contending that something without parallel in Church history took place at Barmen. And, time and again, he strove to make what had been accomplished there a rallying-point for the whole of Reformed Christendom. For it must be emphasized that Barth would not act as if he were striving to form a mere theological or ecclesiastical party within the Church, still less as if he were initiating a quasi- political movement against the Government. In that sense he absolutely abjured the rôle of ecclesiastical statesman. At Barmen, no party was formed, no programme was laid down, no plan of campaign was initiated. A confession was made, an act of obedience was consummated. That was all; and that, in Barth's view, was everything.

By virtue of his theological integrity, Barth became formidable to the authorities of the National Socialist State. He was driven from his professorship in the University of Bonn, and since, even then, he could not be silenced, he was banished from Germany as an undesirable alien. And, as if to make it clear that theologically he was invulnerable, his erstwhile collaborator and fellow worker Gogarten, now became one of his most vigorous opponents, was temporarily installed in his chair at Bonn. In the light of the *dénouement* that followed, Gogarten, in Barth's chair, might be interpreted as a kind of symbol of Barth's vindication. Here, surely, was something in the nature of divine irony!

But the irony was to become more patent still. Gogarten had accused him of plying a "timeless theology", a theology which simply hung in the air, a theology which ignored man as an historical being, a theology which virtually cut the connection between God and man, and which must therefore shut the Church up within herself, and prevent her message from exerting influence on the course of world events, a theology which was a mere dialectical play of concepts. It was, he asserted, when narrowly looked at, a mere "identity theology" of the relation between the perishable and the imperishable for which the present with its events and crises formed an empty space; for, clearly, the dialectic of concepts such as perishable and imperishable was no dialectic of history, but, at best, could only be a dialectic of man conceived of as a being abstracted from history. And yet, all the time Gogarten was uttering these complaints, the theology of Barth was inspiring a most resolute and clear-sighted opposition to the advance of an all-dominating secular tyranny; while Gogarten himself was waiting indecisively on events, now entering and now withdrawing from the German Christian movement. But more was to follow. Barth had declared, in the first volume of his *Prolegomena*, that the real clarifications in the broad field of politics would result from comprehensive clarifications in the theological realm.[1] These clarifications were now becoming

[1] *The Doctrine of the Word of God*, p. xiii

apparent. In an acute study, Barth subjected the whole political theory of National Socialism to a searching theological analysis, exhibiting it as the supreme political question of the day that called for a clear-cut decision on the part of Christendom.[1] In a further study, he examined the relationships between Church and State and related the intricate problems attending these relationships to the Biblical witness to revelation.[2] And when at last war broke out, Barth became something of an œcumenical figure, exercising a kind of apostolate over wide regions, and writing letters to the Churches of Europe which illumined, not simply the spiritual, but the distinctively Christian issues of the war. Thus, there emerged from this peripheral activity of Barth, if we may call it so, the outlines of a theological interpretation of the State, of democracy, and of the idea of law, which was impressive in its weight and its relevance to the situation of the hour. This "timeless theology" seemed strangely timely! This dialectic swinging in empty space seemed to be operating pretty effectively in the crush and conflict of earthly affairs!

All this time, the great Dogmatic work was steadily proceeding. It is now in mid-career and has a long way to go before it finishes its course. Nevertheless, it has attained a certain comprehensiveness in that it has put forth a fully-developed doctrine of God. To this doctrine we shall have presently to give special consideration, for not only does it mark the latest stage of Barth's theology, but it exhibits that theology in a certain completeness which has now only to work itself out in detail. Moreover, this doctrine of God is seen to include a doctrine of man, and a fully articulated doctrine of ethics; for the God who has revealed Himself through His Word is shown to be, in virtue of His very life and history, a God who has eternally bound Himself to man and man to Himself, and who therefore makes claims upon man's life and action, thus determining man's very existence. But, before we address ourselves to an examination of this doctrine, certain observations of a general nature seem to be called for.

And, first of all, this brief sketch which we have given of the development of Barth's undertaking will have failed of its

[1] *Die Kirche und die politische Frage von Leute*   [2] *Church and State*

purpose if it does not promote the conviction that what has taken place is a genuine and perhaps decisive spiritual movement. Beginning as a kind of "marginal note" to all theology, or if higher claims might be made for it, as a "corrective theology", Barthianism, if we may use a term abhorred by Barth himself, has moved steadily forward in the direction of a genuinely theological clarification on a broad front, and has crystallized itself into a vast theological construction. And this it has done, not through some purely logical necessity, for there were many who accepted the "marginal note" and the "corrective" who yet have taken a direction wholly different from that of Barth. One thinks, for example, of Tillich. Barth was forced into the work of theological construction by no mere logical compulsion, but through his recognition of the fact that he had a Lord, and that his thinking must be an act of pure obedience. It was this recognition which made his theology so powerful a factor in the Church struggle against a secular totalitarianism, and which is on the way to making it a genuine contribution to political, social, and ethical theory. No man has properly come to terms with Barth's theology who has not seen it in the light of a spiritual movement, and who does not seek to relate himself in one way or another to this movement. It is not merely an affair of concepts, and it is not to be estimated and adjudged by giving heed to its concepts alone. One had better ask, not simply what one thinks of the concepts as such, but how far the work as a whole may be called an act of obedience. This is the question which will become decisive for this theology.

And the second consideration, which is important here, is that, for the first time in the history of the Christian Church, a theology of vast range, and of striking coherence and clarity, has been built wholly and solely on the foundation of the Word of God as attested in the Biblical witness to revelation. By the confession of Brunner, Barth is the first authoritative Christian teacher who has refused all natural theology. A theology of revelation, which has turned away from all external support, has become an event in the world. This is an objective fact which calls for recognition. It is not, of course, to be maintained that Barth's theology is anything but a human and fallible attempt to subordinate thought to the control of the Word of God alone. All theology must of necessity be a human undertaking, and, like all human undertakings, stands in need of the justification of God. But, here, the intention has been throughout to build upon the foundations supplied by the Biblical witness to revelation and upon no others; and, in the following out of this intention, a massive construction has, as a matter of fact, appeared. Criticism which did not take note of this intention, and which did not examine the construction in its light, would not be a very fruitful thing.

From these considerations it will become clear that no understanding of Barth is possible wherein he is not taken seriously as a theologian. There is a widespread tendency to ignore the theologian while paying lip-service to the "prophet". It is somewhat airily said that he has some value in rescuing the idea of revelation from the relativism in which it was becoming involved through the tendency of modern theology to interpret it by means of norms drawn from history, psychology, and philosophic idealism. In a word, his value is declared to be of a negative nature. But though Barth at first conducted a pretty vigorous campaign against this relativism, his real interests did not lie in this direction. As far back as 1927, Barth said, in referring to his *Commentary on the Epistle to the Romans*: "If my work hitherto has had the effect of being here and there a 'marginal note' and a 'corrective' and must still have this effect, that cannot be my purpose. I am an ordinary theologian." His contention all along has been that only the Word of God can destroy the relativism which was threatening the whole idea of revelation. An independent campaign against relativism could not hope to succeed. A mere prophetic outcry was, in itself, of no avail. Accordingly, Barth disclaims the rôle of the prophet which so many are disposed to assign to him and asks to be judged simply as a theologian. It seems necessary to emphasize this, for even so accomplished a thinker as the late Dr. Edwyn Bevan, in comparing and contrasting Karl Barth with Karl Heim, says: "There is a notable difference of character between the two men. Barth is the prophet, shaking men's hearts by a language which is often defiant and violent in paradox. . . ."[1] These words, strangely enough, appeared after the first volume of Barth's *Prolegomena to Church Dogmatics* had appeared in English. No one is capable of understanding Barth who rests in the view presented of him in Dr. Bevan's words. He must be understood as a theologian or not at all.

There is perhaps in this country a rather too facile opinion that one has settled accounts with Barth and can now afford to pass him by. Again and again criticisms appear to the effect that he is "one-sided"; that he is the advocate of a divine transcendence which leaves no room for immanence; that his work is motivated by a reaction against a self-sufficient humanism and that he has carried his anti-humanism too far; that he empties history of meaning; that his emphasis on the divine sovereignty is of such a kind as to exclude human freedom and responsibility; that he devaluates religious experience; that he is the apostle of irrationalism in religion, and so on. One gets the impression that the theologians who make these charges feel themselves absolved thereby from taking serious account of his positive and constructive theological work. The brief sketch which we shall present in the following chapters of the latest stage of Barth's theological thinking may do something to correct a view of him that is widely current, and to invite attention to the "ordinary theologian".

[1] See Introduction to Heim's *God Transcendent*, Eng. trans., p. v

CHAPTER II

THE DOCTRINE OF GOD (1)

IN an eloquent passage in *Die Lehre von Gott* (*The Doctrine of God*), the volume which advances from Prolegomena or Introduction to the exposition of Christian doctrine proper, Barth declares that everything which Dogmatics has to say in the whole scope of its treatment of divine revelation may be summed up in the simple statement, "God is".[1] When that has been really and truly said: said in such a way that the subject "God" stands forth in its true denotation, and the predicate "is" in its true and rightful meaning, all has been said. The Church's one concern is that this should be said and that this should be heard, namely, "God is"; and Dogmatics which exists simply in the interests of the Church's proclamation can be of service to the Church only as it helps it to say, "God is". It might be thought that there are other concerns and problems with which the Church and Dogmatics must occupy themselves. For example, is there not the age-long problem of the One and the many? How is the existence of beings other than God possible together with His existence? Does not their existence imperil His? Is there not, at any rate, the problem of the absolute and the relative, which is not solved but merely raised by the fact of God's existence? But, no; this problem, like all others, is solved ultimately in the very fact of God's own existence. His existence includes within itself and transcends the distinction between the absolute and the relative. We can speak of no problems, at last, save those which God Himself solves simply in virtue of existing and living as God.

The statement "God is" means that God lives; that He lives means that He wills; that He wills means that what He wills happens. In other words "God is" *in His works and ways*; and I must be able to speak about His works and ways if I am to say that He "is"; for, apart from His works and ways, God "is"

[1] *Dog.*, II, 1, p. 289

not at all. God's works and ways can in no sense be abstracted from His being. They arise in those decisions wherein God determines His own existence. God is not a kind of synthesis of being and action, so that being and action in Him might be held apart and regarded independently of one another. He "is" a life and a history, and His being is "in act". When, therefore, I have said, "God is", I have said what He is and what He has done. And if I have not said what He is and what He has done I have not said, "God is".[1]

Now, the significance of all this will, it is hoped, become clearer as we proceed. We would, however, even at the outset, make the following comment. In this passage to which we have alluded, Barth has summarized the whole of his theology. By this passage he stands or falls. Is he right here or is he wrong? If he is right, criticisms of his theology in detail, and in important detail, may be very relevant; but the structure of his thought will stand. If he is wrong, the whole edifice of his theology collapses. Therefore, we will endeavour to sharpen the issue as acutely as we can. Is it or is it not the case that the God to whom the Bible bears witness, the God of Israel and the Church, the God and Father of our Lord and Saviour Jesus Christ, is wholly given in His great deed of revelation, so given that we can say that He is a God whose being and existence cannot be abstracted from His works and ways, and on the other hand so given that these works and ways cannot be abstracted from His being as their subject?

Let us consider the dilemma into which we are cast if we do, even for one moment, hold apart these two magnitudes, God's "being" and His works and ways. Let us suppose that we can think of God in abstraction from His works and ways, as pure "being" for example, that we can reach the thought of Him as He really is through the concept of "being" in general. Let us suppose that, following the example of St. Thomas Aquinas, we can, apart from any revelation of God's works and ways, establish by means of logic and reason the existence of God as the *ens realissimum* (the most real being); so that, after having established His existence in this independent fashion, we can now go on to an investigation of His works and ways as

[1] p. 290

given in revelation, thus filling out the formal idea of God as "being" with a material content derived from a consideration of His works and ways. We have first established, let us say, that God is; and we now proceed to establish what He is from what He has done. Our "that" has not included the "what". The "what" must be reached in another way than the "that". But wherein lies the connection between what we have established in the one way, and what in the other? Is it not an act of logical violence to refer both to the same subject? Are we not faced with the question as to whether the works and ways of God have anything but a contingent or even arbitrary connection with His innermost and most real being? He might be in Himself something other than His works and ways. There might be in the heights and depths of His being a vast hinterland to His works and ways. To put it briefly, who or what could guarantee for us that these works and ways *were truly His?* Only if these works and ways be real "moments" within God's own being; only if they be the actualizations of decisions wherein and whereby God lives His own life; only if they be God's own determinations of His life and being can we have any confidence in them as truly His; can we have, indeed, any knowledge of them as His at all. Would the God whose being and doing were fundamentally different things, so that His being could be reached along one line of approach, and His doing along quite another, be the God of whom the Bible speaks, the God whom the Church stands under commission to declare? Would He really be God at all? Would not His being stand under some law that His works and ways should correspond with His being and life? Would it not be necessary to call to our aid some metaphysical principle which could establish the identity of being and doing within the life of God? And would the being of such a god standing under such a law be verily the "being" of God the Lord?

But we must hasten to add that, though God's being cannot be detached from His works and ways, that being is not exhausted in these works and ways. God does not, so to speak, pass into them, as if it were possible by a mere examination of them to establish the reality of His life and being. If that were the case, we should be left with a series of more or less isolated facts and deeds which it would be our task to harmonize and unify. We should have, as it were, to abstract God from His works and ways. But how were that a possible proceeding? Once again we should be faced with the question: what could guarantee for us that these works and ways were truly God's? They can only be established as His in so far as He, their subject, *gives Himself* to be known in them. God can never be simply deduced from His works and ways.

The proposition "God is", to use the Barthian terminology, is an analytic and not a synthetic one. That is to say, it includes within itself not simply God's "being" considered in itself and in isolation from His works and ways, but these works and ways as integral to God's life and being. The God of the Bible is not "being" as such. He "is" a life and a history. He "is" in no sense mere object. He "is" altogether subject. He lives and wills and acts. His "being" cannot be abstracted from His living, willing, and acting; and, therefore, He cannot be known save in and through His living, willing and acting. He cannot be known, that is, save as He reveals Himself; and, as He reveals Himself, so He "is". The statement "God is", from the point of view of every natural theology, every theology holding itself apart from special revelation, would be not an analytic but a synthetic statement. That is to say, the concept of God which would form the content of such a statement would be an abstraction from factors lying within the world of man's common experience. This concept would be reached by the synthesis or combination of understandings and insights reached by objective examination and consideration of these factors. The concept of God would therefore be the goal of human thought and reason, an object at last compassed by the effort and striving of man's mind and reason.

The Christian Church can under no circumstances attribute to God the abstract and objective nature which every synthetic statement that God "is", in a word, every natural theology, would imply. It cannot, that is, think of God as the goal of man's thought and perception, as a reality reached at the end of man's own interpretation of the world of his experience. The god reached in that way is not God, but an idol. The whole existence of the Church is bound up with the analytic character of the statement that God "is". That is to say, the Church's existence is bound up with the postulate that one does not end with God but must begin with Him. No man therefore can say "God is" to himself. The Church cannot say it to itself. No single statement about God, the God who really "is", can be made excepting on the ground that God has spoken first, excepting on the ground of God's own being as manifested and revealed in His works and ways. The Church speaks about God not through the exigencies of thought but through the imperative of command. It will of course recognize that the man to whom God speaks in His Word is a man who cannot extricate himself from the exigencies of thought. He cannot make himself a *tabula rasa* for the Word of God. Man is a living, thinking, acting being and to this living, thinking, acting being the Word of God is addressed. But since the Church really speaks to man about God, since to speak is its commission, the command laid upon it, it can in no sense debate with him about God. That is to say, it cannot treat God as, so to speak, half subject of address to man and half object of man's investigations, but must speak of Him as wholly subject. Were it to attempt the former task—and such an attempt is presupposed in every mediating theology, every theology which seeks to set up a synthesis between revelation and man's natural reason—it would renounce its nature as commissioned, as standing under command, as speaking out of pure obedience. Is not then the man to whom the Word of God is addressed called upon to abdicate as a thinker after all? By no means. Since "God is", in the great analytic and not in the synthetic sense, man is legitimized and justified as thinker before God as he follows out to their conclusions the implications of the Word of God given in revelation. As thinker in this sense he will never be confounded. He will discover the answers to his own questions in himself answering the questions put to him by the Word of God. But theology cannot pursue its way in any anxiety about man as a thinker. It cannot and must not charge itself with man's concerns in this respect. It knows that God has taken upon Himself this anxiety in giving to man His revelation, and that therefore all anxiety on its part is superfluous. Theology, like the Church in general, must "seek first

34

the kingdom of God and His righteousness"; then all other things will be added unto it.

We cannot proceed in our exposition without pausing for a moment to glance at a question which continually arises in some form or other throughout Barth's theology, and to which the same answer is given with ever-mounting weight and momentum. We have spoken of God's works and ways, and we have spoken of them as integral to His life and being. And, of course, we must include in them His works and ways in creation, in history, and in ordinary human experience, as well as in the special action of revelation and reconciliation in Jesus Christ. We cannot think of God as isolated from creation, from history, and from the ordinary life of man. When we speak of Him as Reconciler and Redeemer, we cannot do so in a way which would represent Him as a kind of intruder into the world which He has made. Why then, it will be asked, may we not speak of God as in some sense immediately and directly apprehensible from nature and history and human experience in general? Why must revelation be always thought of as always special, and never as a general and universal thing? Why cannot man, of himself and apart from some special act of God, attain in some measure to the knowledge of God? The question may be put in a still more challenging form. Why cannot God, or why must it be supposed that He will not, and does not, reveal Himself to man through His works and ways in creation, history and human life, apart from His special Word and revelation in Jesus Christ? And why do we insist not only that revelation is special and not general, but that its very potentiality and possibility is to be found in God Himself and not at all in the world?

Now, we certainly do not dream of denying that God can reveal Himself where and when and how He will. We do not assert that God is limited and confined in His revealing activity to any special sphere. But to assert the freedom of God in revelation is one thing, and to declare that nature, history, and human life inasmuch as in these the works and ways of God are operative, possess in themselves, and apart from God's own direct decision and action, revelationary quality and power is quite another. That God can use these things as media of His revelation is true; that there is immanent in them revelationary

35

quality and significance, so that by contemplation of them we could in a systematic way build up a valid theory of revelation, is not true and must roundly be denied. And the denial is made not on the ground of any theory of knowledge, but purely and simply because we are confronted in the Biblical witness, and as the very substance of this witness with the reality named Jesus Christ. Jesus Christ, according to the Biblical witness, is the one Word of God in which man has to put his trust for time and for eternity; the Alpha and Omega of God's relationship to man and man's relationship to God; the one way of God to man which sets aside all the self-chosen ways of man to God. And Jesus, again according to the Biblical witness, has His potentiality and possibility not in the world and not in man, as if He were the highest expression of a divinity latent in these (that is a rationalistic interpretation of Jesus Christ, and it stands in flat contradiction to the Biblical witness), but in God alone. Jesus Christ, moreover, means God's grace to men who are not only creatures but sinners. Jesus Christ is the world's redeemer and that means that He is the world's judge. Jesus Christ is the "new from above", and that means that redemption must be thought of as something absolute, a new creation, and therefore that judgment must be thought of as radical. The fact of Jesus Christ presupposes a fallen world, a world whose relationship to God stands in need of a complete rectification. Jesus Christ means in no sense the deification of man and his world, but their complete de-deification. How then is it possible to claim a direct way of approach from man and his world to God? How can God's revelation of Himself be understood otherwise than as reconciliation and redemption? I have not said "God is", unless I mean that the God and Father of our Lord and Saviour Jesus Christ alone is God. All statements, therefore, purporting to impart the knowledge of God receive their validity only in and through the Word of God in Jesus Christ. Whatever revelation God may give through Nature, history, and experience (and we do not deny that He can and does give such revelation even where man has never heard of Christ), is revelation only in and through its God-established unity and identity with the revelation in Jesus Christ.

The Church, therefore, is bound to the Word of God, whose purport is Jesus Christ. She is so bound to that Word that she can concede nothing as genuine knowledge of God which is not given in that Word; so bound that she must call every god save the God therein given an idol. And she is bound to the Word of God by the Word of God itself. She is bound, not through any scepticism on her part concerning the powers and possibilities of human nature, and not through any pessimistic view of man and man's world which she herself might feel justified in adopting. She is bound through nothing negative, but through a great positive, through divine commandment. She is bound because she has been called into being by the Word of God, is maintained in her existence by that Word, and is authenticated in her speech about God through that Word alone.

We may now proceed to a more detailed description of the doctrine of God as unfolded in Barth's latest volumes. He divides his treatment into four main sections: the knowledge of God; the reality of God; God's election of grace; and God's commandment. Under these four headings the subject of the Church's proclamation and witness receives designation; that is to say, the content of the word "God" is indicated. To this treatment we must now address ourselves.

The Knowledge of God

We begin with an investigation into the question of the knowledge of God. And we must first make it clear that the question from the standpoint of the Church cannot be: is God known, or is God knowable? it can only be how, and how far, is God known and knowable? In other words, the nature of the object after which we are enquiring cannot be left an open question. "It cannot remain withheld of whom or of what we have to think when we enquire about the knowledge of God. We are not free with our question about the knowledge of God, perhaps to think of Him who in the Bible is named God and Lord, but perhaps and just as well of these and those other magnitudes which certainly might be designated and given out as God. We could not just as well enquire after the knowledge of the world ground, or the world soul; of the highest good, or of the supreme value; of the thing in itself, or of the absolute; of fate, or being, or of the idea; or of the unity of being and idea, as of the knowledge of Him who in the Bible is God and Lord. Were we in the matter of the knowledge of God as free to look in the different directions in which these concepts point as in that in which the Biblical concept of God points, then of course the problem of the knowledge of God would have to be formulated quite differently than is here the case. . . . In that case there would be a choice of positions from which it could and must be asked whether here knowledge was real and possible. . . . But the realization of the knowledge of God which here concerns us rests not upon a free choice of this or that object, this or that God. It must be laid down . . . that all which on the ground of free choice is designated as 'God' cannot be God, and that all which on the ground of this presupposition is given out as knowledge of God can be neither actual nor possible. What here occupies us as knowledge of God happens not in free choice but in a quite definite binding. It stands or falls with a definite object which could be no other, which cannot be exchanged for any other or even be associated with it. The knowledge of God which here concerns us is bound to God's word, bound to the God who gives Himself in His word to the Church to be recognized as God."[1]

It might be objected that this amounts to a sheer cutting of the Gordian knot, that the man who raises the question of the knowledge of God is here offered an *ipse dixit*: "Yes, God is known, the Bible and the Church say so." But the objection cannot be sustained. If we are not to take up the standpoint in advance that nothing is known or knowable which does not proceed from the inner dialectic of reason, we have to recognize that reason is determined by its object, and that the nature of the object must prescribe the specific mode of the activity of reason. Certainly reason has here to move in a definite sphere and proceed in a definite way. The mode of apprehension which lays hold of the knowledge of God given in revelation will be one which answers to the object given in revelation. And the object here is unique and incomparable.

[1] pp. 4, 5

38

The object is the Word of God; or, put otherwise, it is the speaking God. Whether that object is real or not cannot be decided in any *a priori* fashion; it can only appear *a posteriori*. Indeed, even to say this is to say too much. The Word of God can only accredit itself as it is heard, as it becomes event. Theology itself cannot demonstrate its reality. But what can be expected of theology is that it should exhibit the kind of rationality which corresponds with the object of its thought; that it should set forth a type of dialectic which is compact, coherent and of its kind satisfying; that, moreover, it should go farther and penetrate deeper than reason on its ordinary levels is capable of doing, and so raise and answer questions which lie beyond the horizon of the ordinary reason, thus creating a crisis in thought to which the ordinary thinker will have sooner or later to relate himself. The Christian theologian proceeds from the presupposition that there is an object of his thought, that this object is given; and he goes on his way without stopping to justify his undertaking before the bar of secular science, but confident that this undertaking will justify itself. This object cannot be religion in general, religion as a subject of impartial investigation, religion as a mere human fact, religion as an historical or psychological phenomenon to which one is free to relate oneself one way or the other. That is not the object with which the theologian is confronted in the Biblical witness to revelation and in the proclamation of the Christian Church. Here man stands under command and his task is one of commission. Here thought moves in a direction which it does not choose, but which is chosen for it. But this means no sacrifice of the intellect. Paradoxically, it is the much lauded free thought, the thought which is not bound to any object, but which assumes that it must choose its own object, which leads into a sea of uncertainties from which it can only extricate itself by some sacrifice of the intellect.[1] The uniqueness of the knowledge of the God of whom revelation speaks is that it is knowledge which wholly determines the knower, knowledge which therefore leads to certainty, and which has accordingly no need of that *salto mortale*, the sacrifice of the intellect.

[1] pp. 6, 7

The knowledge of God given in revelation is knowledge of a subject which, in order that it may become apprehensible to men, takes upon itself the form of an object.[1] God Himself, according to the witness of the Bible, is pure subject. He is the Lord. He is the great "I" on whom our human "I" depends and from whom it derives. But in order to make Himself known to us men He objectifies Himself to us, meets us on our own plane, thus as another man; for all knowledge implies an object. We do not encounter Him by diving down into the depths of our own nature and spirit, as if He were the extension and prolongation of our own being. That way, the mystic way, could be no real encounter. It would not be the meeting of a real "I" with a real "Thou". But God, in order that we may encounter Him as another than ourselves, thus as an object of our knowledge, meets us as another man, the man Jesus. In Jesus, man stands before God and God stands before man. But all the time God does not cease to be Himself; does not, that is, cease to be subject, the Lord. God does not become object in the sense that He delivers Himself over into men's hands, thus putting Himself at the disposal of their free investigation. Thus, God is not known by means of direct knowledge of the man Jesus; is not known, that is, as Jesus is made the subject of historical or psychological enquiry. He does not, as it were, pass over into the man Jesus, so that as God, as subject, as the Lord, He ceases to be. In objectifying Himself, He veils Himself as subject, and in such self-veiling He reveals Himself. That is to say, His objectifying of Himself never ceases to be *action*; it never passes into an object abstracted from the divine action. It never ceases to be self-giving, and that which is given cannot be held apart from the person and action of the giver. And this giving, this action, calls for a corresponding action on the part of man; calls for a receiving and an appropriating answering in its human way to the self-giving of God. The knowledge of God is therefore a faith knowledge. It is no mere mastering by the mind of an object, but the mastering of the mind by a subject which moves and acts in the object presented to the mind. It is the personal response of man to the God who gives Himself in His Word.

[1] p. 8

This faith knowledge is accordingly an *obedience*. The obedience is not merely something which follows from the act of faith, and which therefore belongs to man's free choice and determination. The faith which is knowledge of God is, as such, obedience to God's Word; and, apart from this faith, there is no obedience on the part of man.

The content of this faith knowledge of God is describable in a two-fold way. First, it is "the existence of One whom man *may* love above all things and whom therefore he *must* fear".[1] Man may love Him, for God gives Himself to man as One who will not be without him. And man must fear Him, for He confronts man as another than himself and claiming his obedience, and thus threatening man's independent existence. Apart from this love and this fear there is no knowledge of God. And, secondly, it is "the existence of One who remains a mystery to man because He has made Himself so clear and certain."[2] Inasmuch as God veils Himself in the object in which He presents Himself to man, inasmuch as He ever remains subject, He remains the great secret and mystery. But inasmuch as it is verily Himself who is disclosed to man in the object that confronts him, He makes Himself clear and certain. Man has not to fear that God may be in Himself something other than what He is in His revelation. It is only by the use of these antitheses "love" and "fear", "mystery" and "clearness and certainty" that we can assure ourselves that we are really speaking of God, of the God of revelation. An existence which did not demand these antitheses would be in the last resort a mere prolongation of man and man's world, and on that account could not be man's and the world's absolute Lord.

Having established the fact that the God of whom the Bible and the Church speak is really known, we have to proceed to a further enquiry. We have to ask how comes it to pass that God *can* be known; in other words, what is the divine ground of the possibility of the knowledge of Him?[3] This divine ground must be brought into view, in order that the door may be closed against the supposition that behind the actual knowledge of God given in revelation there might be a kind of empty

[1] p. 34   [2] p. 40   [3] p. 68

space which could be filled in by some natural knowledge of Him. Unless not merely the *fact*, but also the *possibility* of the fact, is rooted in God's own life and being, the danger of a natural theology overlapping the theology of revelation and threatening to bring it to the ground is ever present.

The necessity of our enquiry about the possibility of the knowledge of God is created by the fact that natural theology is actually on the field, thus compelling the theology of revelation to take note of its claims and to define its position in relation to those claims. But here a word of caution is needed. It is not the concern of the Church and it can never be the business of the theologian to conduct a direct campaign against natural theology. Such a campaign could not possibly succeed. For the striving after a natural theology, after a knowledge of God from man's own centre, springs inevitably, and but for the grace of God irresistibly, out of man's own vitality.[1] It is man's effort, an effort involved in his unredeemed existence, to assure himself in face of his world, to make himself secure in the midst of his life, to obtain for himself standing-ground as an independent and self-contained reality in the scheme of things. By striving out of his own powers and insights to attain to knowledge of God, man seeks to establish himself over against his world, seeks to gain a footing in ultimate reality. Any direct attack from the side of the Church against natural theology is felt to be an attack against man's very existence.

It is not within the competence, and should not be within the competence, of any theology as such to make this attack successfully. Only God Himself, in His actual work of revelation, only His Word and Spirit can "unsecure" man, can open his eyes to the fact that the ground which he seeks to obtain for himself is no ground at all but only shifting sand. The very account which we have given of natural theology, namely, that it springs out of man's own vitality, is one which springs from revelation itself. Simply as our account it is open to question. How then is it possible to meet natural theology on its own ground and there to overthrow it? What would an effort of this kind be but an attempt of one theory of knowledge to overthrow another? What is required of the Church

[1] pp. 93, 185

42

theologian, therefore, is not that he should set out on a direct crusade against natural theology, but that, bound to the Word of God and following the direction of that Word, he should seek to ground the possibility of the knowledge of God wholly and solely in God Himself.

We take the necessary step forward when we speak of a readiness or openness of God for man, and of a corresponding readiness or openness of man for God.[1] What is the nature of this twofold openness? It will be clear from all that has been said that we cannot speak of a natural and self-existing openness of man for God. Man's openness for God is wholly grounded in God's openness for man; it is a participation in that openness. But the ground of this openness of God for man lies in the fact that He is open to Himself. To put it otherwise: God can objectify Himself to man in order to be known by him, because He is already and in His own being object to Himself, the Father to the Son through the Holy Spirit. The Trinitarian conception of God which is involved in the Biblical witness speaks of a divine subject which, as such, is object to itself; of an internal self-communion and self-communication which eternally is. Knowability therefore belongs to the very nature of God. But that does not mean that God is under some kind of *necessity* to make Himself knowable to us. His becoming an object of knowledge to us is grounded in His good pleasure alone. It is, so to speak, a pure overflow of that self-communion and self-communication which is ever going on within God's own life and into which we are gathered through His grace. But, because it is this, we are precluded from the attempt to establish a knowledge of God from the side of natural theology. We know of no possibility of such knowledge, of no empty space behind the knowledge of God given in revelation which we might fill in from our side. Every hypothetical empty space is already filled in that knowledge of God by us which is an overflow of God's own knowledge of Himself.

But the question still remains, how far this openness of God for man means an openness of man for God. Here we shall have to speak of a correspondence between man's knowledge of God as apprehended by faith and God's giving of Himself in

[1] p. 70

revelation; between the human action of receiving God's Word and the divine action in giving it. Of a correspondence, we shall say; not of an equivalence. There will be all the inequality which exists between God and man, between the Creator and the creature; and, above all, between the Holy and the sinful. Of an *analogia entis* (analogy of being) existing between God and man on the basis of which something in the nature of an equivalence between the openness of God for man and that of man for God might be established, there can be no speech. But we may speak of an analogy of faith. We may say that the human decision in which the act of faith is consummated is, despite the fact that it is only human, in vital correspondence with the divine decision consummated in the divine act of revelation. We may even speak, and indeed we must speak, of a perfection of the knowledge of God given to faith.

> *A perfect God is He*
> *And He is wholly ours.*

Faith, in so far as it is really faith, is perfect knowledge of God. By perfect we mean here wholly trustworthy, completely sure and certain, with a trustworthiness and a certainty which correspond to God's own knowledge of Himself. A knowledge which was not perfect in this sense would not be knowledge of God. It would not apprehend God Himself in His Word; it would not participate in God's own openness to Himself. It cannot be sufficiently emphasized that the faith which corresponds to the knowledge of God, knows *God*; not merely things about God, but God as He really is, God in His true being; and that no other knowledge than the knowledge of faith does this. Certainly the concepts by means of which faith seeks to set out its knowledge of God are in themselves wholly inadequate. Being the concepts of our human thinking they are even perverted and in themselves false. But inasmuch as they are used in the service of faith, they are laid hold of by the Word of God, like our human nature in general, and are validated as instruments of the divine revelation.

The way of faith is, therefore, the way which the Church has to take; and faith, though it is called forth by the action of

God in revelation, and may therefore rightly be called a gift, is none the less a human decision and a human action. And since it is an action from the side of man, it has a *goal* and an *object*. It not only starts from the knowledge of God, it presses forward to that knowledge. The man of faith, just because he has been found by God, is continually seeking God. We must, therefore, think of the knowledge of God not only as the presupposition but also as the *goal* of Christian doctrine.[1] Our thought has to travel not only along the way from God to man, but also along the way from man to God. But, even when we travel along this latter way, we cannot step off the path that is laid down by God as He comes to man in revelation.[2] Proceeding along this path we shall say that faith reaches its true goal in the knowledge of God, as man's thinking and speaking are taken in claim by the Word of God, as this thinking and speaking are undertaken in responsibility to that Word and to that alone.[3] We shall, furthermore, say that man in all this thinking and speaking advances by way of humility, thankfulness, awe, and joy.[4] In saying this we are pointing to those determinations of man's existence which are in vital correspondence with the self-determinations of God's own existence in the act of giving to man His revelation of Himself. As man allows himself to be taken in claim by the Word of God, as he moves forward in humility, thankfulness, awe, and joy, he travels along the road which leads to the knowledge of God. He goes forward from faith to faith.

But what can assure us that we are really taking the way of faith and that therefore what we take to be knowledge of God is this indeed? In other words, what can assure us that what we call our faith has been a real response to a real Word of God? From one point of view, the question need not detain us. We could not seek to assure ourselves by attempting to test the reality of our faith according to any criterion standing outside the sphere of faith. We could not take up some neutral position from which, as spectators, we might survey faith and pass judgment upon it. There is no certainty outside faith which could lend certainty to faith. Faith, if it be real, cannot, so to speak, stop being faith in order to assure itself that it is really faith and

[1] p. 229   [2] p. 235   [3] p. 237   [4] p. 240 ff.

thus has a real object. It is faith, and faith alone, that lays hold of its object; and it must lose its object directly it becomes anything else. But, necessary as this reminder is, it does not truly answer our question. The whole procedure of our thought has been a movement in a circle. We have advanced from the knowledge of God as presupposition to the knowledge of Him as a conclusion. Certainly we have appealed to revelation throughout. But, simply because we have made this appeal, we have not thereby established the fact that our circle has been a circle of truth. Might it not have been a vicious circle? A movement of thought is in itself no more than a movement of thought.[1] It cannot of itself bring either revelation or faith on the field. If revelation be a decision of God, then the question as to the reality of our faith must be left to His decision. In other words, this question cannot be one which we put to ourselves; it can only be one which we allow to be put to us by God. In other words, again, our faith simply as ours, simply as a human activity, continually stands under God's judgment. The assurance which we seek cannot be found in any movement of our thought, it can only be found where our thought comes to an end in pointing to His *promise*. And that point is Jesus Christ.[2] In the Cross of Christ, man is "unsured" in order that in His Resurrection he may be "assured" in a new and divine way. In the Cross, God takes from man all confidence in his very faith, considered as a human act and work, in order in the Resurrection to give him back his faith again; but, this time, not as a human act and work but as a divine gift. Man comes to rest, therefore, not in his faith, as such, but in the object of that faith. He looks away from his own faith to the faith of Jesus Christ. He recognizes that the true subject of the knowledge of God is not himself but Jesus Christ, and he sees his own faith united with the faith of Jesus Christ by God's own direct deed of grace. His confidence, therefore, is not that He knows God, but that He is known by God. And he knows that in this confidence he will never be confounded.

[1] p. 278   [2] p. 283

46

CHAPTER III

THE DOCTRINE OF GOD (2)

The Reality of God

WE pass now from the consideration of the knowledge of God
to a closer consideration of Him who acts as subject in that
knowledge, God Himself in His reality. Barth prefers to speak
of the "reality" rather than of the "being" of God, because
"our first and deciding interpretation of the sentence 'God is'
must be 'God is who He is in the act of His revelation.' "[1]
The word reality thus gathers together being and action,
whereas the word "being" in itself would tear these two things
apart. God's revelation of Himself is, as we have seen, not
something which could be held apart from His being and life.
It is a self-determination of that being and life. We cannot deal
with God's revelation and God's essential being as with two
independent themes. In dealing with His revelation we are
dealing with His being, and in dealing with His being we are
dealing with His revelation.

In revelation, then, we have to do with an act; and, since
it is God's act, it is an act which can in no wise be "transcended".
Though it took place on the field of time, and so in past history,
it abides as an event of God's own life and history, a "moment"
in His "being" as God, so that wherever God is present, the
reality and power of this event is present also. God acts upon
the world in and through this event. "Jesus Christ is the same
yesterday, to-day, yea and for ever. Here there is no surmounting, no surpassing, no standing outside. It is always a matter
of the birth, death, and resurrection of Jesus Christ, always of
His justification of faith, always of His ruling of the Church,
always of His return, and so of Him as our hope. . . . And
precisely in this event is God who He is . . . God is the Lord
acting in this event. We emphasize, above all, *acting*. In seeking
and finding God in His revelation we cannot pass over God's

[1] p. 293

47

acting to a non-acting God. Not only because we ourselves could not do this, but because there is no 'over' or 'outside' to this divine acting. . . . We are concerned with the 'being' of God, but precisely in view of His 'being' is the word 'act' or 'event' a last word, not to be surpassed or put in question. The Godhead of God right to its deepest depths consists in this, that it is event: not any event, not event in general, but the event of His action in which we in God's revelation are involved."[1]

The Divine act in which the being and nature of God are expressed, and from which they cannot be severed is the act in which God seeks and creates fellowship between Himself and us. This fellowship is, as it were, an overflow of the fellowship in which God lives His own life, the Father with the Son and the Son with the Father in the Holy Spirit. It is not as if God needed fellowship with us. Already He possesses it in Himself. But in and through His good pleasure He allows it to overflow to us. He can do this; He can create fellowship with beings other than Himself, because He is in Himself fellowship. A seeking and creating of fellowship is manifestly the creation, the setting up and the maintaining of a reality other than God's own. But this is raised to a higher power in the work of revelation, which is not merely the continuation of creation, but its surpassing; for this work of revelation is identical with the reconciliation of sinful man in the incarnation, death and resurrection of the Son of God. And this seeking and shaping of fellowship reaches its crown and consummation in the determination of the reconciled man for eternal redemption and life. All this which God does, He "is". He will not be Himself otherwise than in this relation. We have certainly to remind ourselves that this relation is not an unequivocal one. It includes the contrast between Creator and creature. It also includes and establishes God's wrath and conflict with sin. There is death and hell in this relation as well as life and heaven. But in all that, it will still be this relation. When God judges and condemns, it is still His own whom He judges and condemns. There is no neutrality of God as over against man, and no neutrality of man as over against God. God has eternally bound Himself to man in His Word, even as He created him through

[1] p. 294

that Word, and in this binding He lives His own life and determines His own being.

Now that being so, we cannot describe or define the being of God otherwise than thus: "God is the loving in freedom."[1] In speaking of the loving in freedom we have spoken of God Himself, His essential Godhead. Again we must emphasize that we do not mean that God is a being to whose essential nature we may add the contingent fact that He loves in freedom. This fact is in no sense contingent, is in no sense separable from the essential nature of God. Apart from the loving in freedom, there is no being of God. God does not merely love, He is love, and apart from His love He "is" not at all. But when we say that God is love, we must not turn the sentence round and say that love is God, as if we could take love as a general concept with the meaning of which we were already familiar, and apply it forthwith to God. We must remember that the subject, God, gives the whole content to the predicate, love. In other words the meaning of the word love as applied to God derives entirely from God's action in revelation. We learn what God's love is from His Word which is Jesus Christ, and not from ourselves. And we must further remember that the man who is the object of God's love in no way determines that God should be loving. How could he since the determining object of the love of God eternally exists within God's own being? We must therefore speak of God's freedom in speaking of God's love.

In speaking of God's freedom we designate His being as wholly moved through itself.[2] It is highly important to give this positive significance to the freedom of God. Too often this freedom has been defined as mere independence of all that is not God Himself. Certainly it is that, but, in itself, that designates simply a negative, and the conception of God is thereby brought too near to that of the "unmoved mover" of ancient classical thought. God is not the unmoved; how could He be since He is the living God, the God who is what He is in action. God is He who is moved through Himself. The freedom of God thus understood points to the possibility of God binding Himself to another than Himself.

[1] p. 288   [2] pp. 338 ff.

If, then, we are to take the way of revelation, we shall need the two words "love" and "freedom" for the designation of the being of God, and we shall recognize that these two words express, so far as human words can, the whole essence and reality of God. God "is" the loving in freedom. All else that we may say about Him will be but description of this love and freedom as these unfold themselves and manifest themselves in God's life and action.

The Perfections (Attributes) of God

It is necessary to keep this in mind as we turn now to the consideration of what are generally known as the divine attributes, or, as Barth prefers to call them, the Divine perfections. As we follow the guidance of revelation we are confronted with a wealth of divine attributes or perfections in which the nature of God is, as it were, unfolded. God discloses Himself to us in revelation, and that means He lives His life as God in a fullness of attributes which are related to one another in such a way that we have continually to pass from the one to the other if we are to understand each one of them aright.

Theologians have often divided these attributes into two main classes, the metaphysical and the moral. Thus, such attributes as omnipotence, omnipresence, eternity, and the like, were classified as metaphysical; while holiness, grace, mercy, patience, and so on, were called moral. The metaphysical attributes were regarded as inhering in God's essential nature, His being in itself; while the moral were looked upon as arising from His relation to the world, and, therefore, in some sense less real than the metaphysical. It is, however, ambiguous and even dangerous to contrast such terms as metaphysical and moral in relation to God. For there are no moral attributes of God which are not as such metaphysical, and there are no metaphysical but which in the same way are moral. In each of the attributes, whether moral or metaphysical, the one God who is "the loving in freedom" lives His life in full perfection. When we say that God is good, we must put full weight on the word "is". We speak of His "being" in speaking of His goodness.

But, once more, when we say that God is good, we must put full weight on the word "good". We speak of His goodness in speaking of His "being". Such contrasted terms as moral and metaphysical derive their whole significance from the God who is their subject, and therefore in the last resort they cannot be contrasted. All that we can rightly mean when we distinguish between moral and metaphysical in this region is that the whole content of the moral attributes is to be found in the nature and life of God Himself and that therefore this content is apprehended only through revelation. God's goodness is *His* goodness, and not some general idea of goodness which we might out of ourselves take up and apply to Him.

Barth therefore departs from the old classification and speaks rather of the perfections of the divine love and the perfections of the divine freedom. This division has the merit of avoiding the suggestion that there are some attributes which do not inhere in the divine being itself but which only arise through the relation of God to beings other than Himself; and it makes unambiguously clear the fact that the God who gives Himself to be known in His revelation is none other than God as He is in Himself. God's love and God's freedom; or, to put it otherwise, God as He relates Himself to us and God as He is in Himself, are in no way to be separated from one another, and treated apart from one another. When we speak of His love we must immediately pass to His freedom, that is, to Himself, and when we speak of His freedom we must immediately pass to His love. But there are some attributes which we describe best by beginning with the idea of His love, and there are some which we describe best by proceeding in the opposite direction.

It conduces most to clearness if, in treating of the Divine attributes or perfections, we set out from the consideration of God's love; for the being of God is, as we have seen, a being in action, the action of revelation, and unless we establish the connection of all the attributes with God's act of revelation, that is, with His love, we let slip our grasp of their true subject. If we start with God's freedom, or, to use the old nomenclature, with the metaphysical attributes, we shall run the risk of thinking of God's "being" in the abstract, and so of falling under the sway of philosophical categories. The great achievement of Barth in this region is his demonstration that all the attributes of God, even such apparently "metaphysical" ones as almightiness, omnipresence, and the like are radii from the one centre of His love.

The Perfections of God's Love

Following the indications given in the scriptural witness to revelation, we shall speak of the attributes of the divine love as grace, mercy, and patience: and for the true understanding of these we shall have to pass over to His holiness, righteousness, and wisdom, in which the *freedom* in that love makes its appearance.[1]

(a) Grace and Holiness

We begin with grace. The word grace fixes our thought more definitely than any other on the fact that we have to do with a love which is in no sense conditioned by the creature. Man who is the object of the divine love is not worthy of it; is, indeed, wholly, unworthy. God is gracious to man because He is in Himself grace.[2] Grace is no third term between God and man, no gift which could be detached from the giver; it is first and foremost an inner being and self-relation of God Himself.[3] In His grace, God comes down, as it were, from His own height. He condescends to man. And He can do this because He is Himself truly high and above man. This condescension, this self-descent of God from His heights is His grace. It might be thought, then, that we could not speak of God as being in Himself grace, because there is in Him no possibility of condescension, no stooping from His own height, and no opposition to be overcome as in the case of sinful man. That is, of course, true in so far as the *form* of grace is concerned. With reference to man, grace takes the form of condescension. But this form has its counterpart in God's own being, though the form which it takes there is hidden from our understanding.[4] All we can do in this region is to point to the inner relations subsisting within the Triune being of God, wherein a free movement of love constitutes the divine life. Had Barth been familiar with the thought of the late Dr. P. T. Forsyth he might

[1] p. 394   [2] p. 401   [3] p. 397   [4] p. 401

have pointed rather more explicitly to the relationship of subordination of the Son to the Father, a subordination which in no way involves inferiority. There is, so to speak, an upper and a lower within the being of God, which is the ground of the possibility of a descent from God to man.

To understand grace aright we must have recourse to the thought of holiness in which the *subject* of grace, God Himself, becomes explicit. The holiness of God is not something additional to His grace, something with which His grace needs to be reconciled. We have spoken of the whole Godhead when we have spoken of grace.[1] Could we by means of our language and in terms of our apprehension speak adequately of God's grace there would be no need of passing on to speak of His holiness. But our apprehension of God's truth must be a moving apprehension, and it can only be this by availing itself of terms which in our thought have distinct but connected connotation.

That which is common to the ideas of grace and holiness is that both point to the height of God, His complete otherness and superiority in relation to all that is not Himself, an otherness and superiority which is in no way abated by His love.[2] In that God is gracious, He does not cease to be true to Himself. He does not ignore or pass by or simply beat down the opposition of the creature and the sinner. His grace, while coming down to the sinner in favour, judges and condemns his sin. The opposition between God and the sinner is established in the very act of being overcome. "God is holy in that His grace is judgment, but also His judgment grace."[3]

(b) Mercy and Righteousness

But our thought must continue in movement and so we now return to the theme of God's love in order to give it a further delimitation. We speak now of mercy or compassion. Here we encounter the positive quality of God's stooping to man. God takes man's need and misery, and especially the need and misery caused by man's sin, into His own heart. He demonstrates that He does not will this need and misery but that He wills to remove it. The compassion of God means that He has a heart: no, that He *is* a heart. God not only knows and wills; He feels.

[1] p. 402   [2] p. 404   [3] p. 408

53

And His feeling is no weak and passive thing, but a strong and active thing. It is not just something that happens to God, it is a movement of His own life and being. It must therefore be understood in connection with His righteousness. In speaking here of righteousness we point to the fact that in showing mercy and compassion God does that which is worthy of Himself; that in taking into His own heart the need and misery caused by man's sin God guards and demonstrates His own absolute worthiness. Man is, indeed, ready enough on occasion to receive pity and compassion merely as such, but he will not allow God to take his need and distress into His own heart. He resists not mercy, as such, but the subject of that mercy, God; and so he resists the mercy of God. His feeling sets itself against God's feeling. Therefore the feeling of God opposes the feeling of man. It becomes wrath, and because it is the feeling of strength and not of weakness, the feeling which moves in action, it becomes burning wrath.[1] Nevertheless, it does not cease to be mercy and compassion. God does not allow His wrath to blaze forth on man, but in His freedom places Himself in man's stead, identifies Himself with man's distress, and so allows His wrath to fall upon Himself, to enter as affliction into His own life and being.

We are here brought face to face with the thought of the substitutionary sufferings of Christ on man's behalf; and Barth sketches in brief an aspect of the divine atonement of great importance. The significant thing about it in this connection is that he shows that a true understanding of the substitutionary sufferings of Christ effectively disposes of the objection that the guilty is here made to shelter behind the sufferings of the innocent. Since it is God Himself who, in Jesus Christ, puts Himself in man's place and identifies Himself with man's case, there can be no thought of any such sheltering. On the contrary, man is taken out of every shelter, every hiding-place, and brought face to face with God Himself in His pity and compassion.[2] Of course, if what took place in the event of the Cross of Christ were merely a case of human suffering, there would be every ground for the objection that the substitution of Christ for us involved our sheltering behind an innocent man. But we

[1] p. 421   [2] p. 453

have not a case of the innocent suffering for the guilty, as that is generally understood; and we entirely misapprehend the atonement if we interpret it under any such general category. Immense confusion has been caused by attempting to range the atonement in a kind of general scheme; by regarding it as an illustration of the law that in such a world as this, redemption comes by the suffering of the innocent for the guilty. If there is such a law, it is certainly not a divine law. It is not right, but terribly wrong, that the innocent should have to suffer for the guilty. The canonizing of such a law, if we may so speak, is a perverted piece of sentiment; not to say a miserable piece of idolatry. The atonement is no illustration of a general law, and to rationalize it after that fashion is a declining from the dialectic of faith to that of natural theology. The atonement can be illustrated by no law; it can only be clarified from the standpoint of the grace and mercy of God, which is not grace and mercy in general, but that kind of grace and mercy in which a great and divine worth and righteousness is demonstrated and established.

(c) Patience and Wisdom

But our thinking must move on to a further delimiting of the love of God. We speak now of the attributes of patience and wisdom. In speaking of the patience of God we point to the fact that God gives man time and space to develop his own life in order that man may turn to Him in repentance and obedience. "Patience is there, where one gives to another, in accordance with a definite purpose, space and time, where one is waiting upon another, allows that other to be."[1] We may well ask whether that purpose is ever truly realized. Does a real repentance and a real obedience corresponding to the patience of God ever take place? Is not the divine patience the outcome of a divine delusion?[2] We may perhaps put the matter somewhat differently and ask: are there any signs that history is moving to a divine goal; any signs that a divine purpose is being realized in the course of man's life in space and time? Of ourselves, we could give no answer to this question. Of ourselves, we should have to say that there is no clear and unambiguous

---

[1] p. 459   [2] pp. 467 ff.

indication that God was not enduring the existence of man in vain. But we may not speak out of ourselves but only out of the event of revelation in Jesus Christ. And here we are referred, not to any indications of repentance and obedience which we might perceive as we survey the course of the world's history, but to the obedience of Christ. In the Word that became flesh, became creature, God goes the whole way with man, and, as it were, overtakes him. Man's repentance and obedience are consummated in the event of Jesus Christ. In Him the purpose of God with man's life is perfectly realized through God's own deed of love for men. Certainly the consummation of this purpose supplies no metaphysic of history, but it offers a sure ground of assurance and trust that God's purpose with history will be secured either in grace or in judgment. Man is not left to himself in that he is permitted to live his own life. History is not left to itself in that it is allowed to proceed on its way. The patience of God is not weakness but power.

Incidentally, it may be noted that the divine attribute of patience disqualifies any mystic way of approach to the knowledge of God. It is of the essence of all mysticism that it strives to annihilate time and to sink into a timeless eternity. The God of mysticism is an "impatient" God. Mysticism has no real use for time. It asserts the fundamental identity of man and God, time and eternity. It cannot at last permit the thought that God permits a wholly other than Himself to exist along with His own existence.[1]

The thought of God's patience is apprehensible only in connection with that of His wisdom. Here, once more, we are directed to Him who is the subject of this patience. God is patient because He is wise; indeed, because He is Himself the true wisdom and reason; patient because He knows why, and for what, He is what He is, and does what He does. There is no caprice in God, no irrationality. God is the source and fount of all ordering, all meaning, all true and real planning.[2] Were He not in Himself wise, how should we know that His patience, and not His patience only, but also His grace, holiness, mercy, and righteousness were not, so to speak, accidental things, things that conceivably might not be? But God is not the great

[1] p. 460   [2] pp. 477 ff.

Irrational. That does not mean that our human reason as such, our reason acting autonomously, and independently of the Word of God, is a divine thing. Neither does it mean that God is the immanent reason of the world. The world has meaning as it *gets* meaning from Him who, above all, has meaning and is meaning. Reason in the true sense is identical with those decisions and acts in which God lives His own life, in which God is what He is; and supremely with that act and decision in which God is patient, in which He allows another existence than His own to be, in which He gives to this other existence space and time in order that it may turn to Him and so find reason and meaning in itself. We may say that the true reason or wisdom is rooted in the unfolding of God's own life and being in the inner connections between His attributes or perfections, for from these the world derives its being and the determinations which govern its life and history. This wisdom is the true philosophy "a philosophy which is not to be deduced from the universe as such, or from the nature of man, but is only to be understood through God's own word as God's own word."[1]

The Perfections of the Divine Freedom

Having proceeded on our way so far, we find ourselves under the necessity of allowing our thought to turn round and move in the reverse direction. We have spoken of the attributes, or perfections of God's love. For the true understanding of these we have been compelled to make a continual transition to the thought of His freedom. We have been compelled, that is, to pass from the attributes or qualities in themselves to Him who is their subject. Only so were we guarded from the danger of interpreting these attributes from the standpoint of general ideas, and so making a god in our own image. When we have said that God is gracious, merciful, and patient, we have had continually to ask, who is He of whom such things are said; and thus in immediate connection with these attributes we have had to speak of God's holiness, righteousness and wisdom. But now we must begin again, this time with those attributes which make explicit the *freedom* of God; and, in

[1] p. 487

order to understand these aright, we shall have continually to pass to the connections of these with His *love*. Our thought throughout is governed by the consideration that from the standpoint of the Word of God we can make no statement about the being of God that does not derive from His action in revelation, and no statement about God's action which does not bring immediately on the field the being of Him who is the subject of that action. Our thought about God can never be free thought; it must ever remain thought which is bound to its object. And the object to which our thought is bound is God in action. Once let "God" and "action" be separated in thought and "God" disappears. We are then left with a mere God-idea or concept which from the point of view of revelation can claim no validity, which indeed must be overthrown as an idol.

Barth characterizes the attributes or perfections of the freedom of God thus: "the divinity of God's freedom consists and is established in this, that God is in Himself and in all His works, one, permanent, and eternal, and therewith also omnipresent, almighty, and glorious."[1] The words one, permanent, and eternal, point specifically to the *freedom* of God in His love; the words omnipresent, almighty, and glorious, to the *love* of God in His freedom.

(a) Oneness and Omnipresence

We begin with the oneness of God. And we mean by that, first, that God is single and unique; that He is in no way comparable to any existence other than Himself. And, secondly, we mean that He is simple, that is, indivisible; that He is in no sense a synthesis of powers and realities which might be thought of as essential to His nature.[2] In all the wealth of His perfections He is simply Himself. No one of these perfections exists without all the others, can be understood in isolation from all the others, or in isolation from Himself as their subject. The decisive thing about God's oneness is that it cannot be compared with any other kind of oneness. Every other oneness is a special instance among other instances comparable with a species belonging to some genus.

[1] p. 495   [2] p. 498

The mere idea of monotheism does not convey the meaning of the oneness of God. Monotheism of a kind underlies the whole of heathen religion, and reaches its high point in Mohammedanism, which is simply the apotheosis and concentration of heathenism in that it is the reduction of the great powers of the world to a common denominator which is styled the one God. The roots of monotheism as a general idea are to be found in man's absolutizing of himself. Either he takes the idea of individuality as he finds it in himself and ascribes to it divinity, or else, despairing of his individuality, as such, he seeks to merge it in a higher existence in which it will lose its limitations. Thus, in the higher regions of thought, men hypostatize reason, or fate, or some such entity, and seek to raise it to highest terms by endowing it with personal significance and potency. But one does not escape from heathenism or reach the oneness of God by canonizing the number one.[1]

The oneness of the true God is not a mathematical term. "The knowledge of it is in no sense the result of man's perception or construction but of the *meeting* between God and man."[2] In that meeting a real "I" confronts a real "Thou". The oneness of God is given in *event* and not in any idea. None of the other kinds of oneness at which we have glanced contains within itself the fact of this meeting, this event. With them all, the oneness is dependent upon and derived from man and man's world. But God's oneness is a oneness set over against and distinguished from man and man's world in their totality. It is the oneness of pure subject which has nothing in common with the differentiation and multifariousness of all that is objective. The oneness therefore cannot be understood apart from the free love of God; apart from the act in which God meets man, becomes present to him, chooses him for fellowship with Himself.

Now the thought of the oneness of God is enlarged and deepened by that of His omnipresence. Omnipresence is undoubtedly an aspect of the freedom of God. "It is the sovereignty in which He ... existing and acting in the way that corresponds to His nature is present to everything which is not Himself."[3] But the omnipresence of God is, above all, the

[1] pp. 504 f.   [2] p. 507   [3] pp. 519 f.

omnipresence of His love. God in the freedom of His love allows that which is other than Himself to *co-exist* with Himself. This co-existence of His with that which is not Himself, with the creature, has its ground of possibility in the fact that God is in Himself the co-existing, the Triune God. The otherness of the created world to God cannot mean its separation from Him. Since the creation is His creation, its otherness from Him is His otherness from it; that is to say, it arises and is maintained in a decision and determination of His own being. Creation implies both farness and nearness, but these are God's farness and nearness. Both the farness and the nearness are related to God, and He is present though in different ways in both. We thus arrive at the following definition of space: "Space is the form of the creation by which it happens that the creation as a reality different from God can be the object of His love."[1] In order that God may be omnipresent externally, omnipresent to that which is outside Himself, there is need of space as a form of the creation.

In interpreting the omnipresence of God in terms of His love (the love in His freedom) Barth stands apart from the traditional Dogmatic. This connected together the omnipresence of God with His eternity, on the ground that the former brought out His relation to space and the latter His relation to time. Both concepts were derived from the idea of infinity as a general notion. God was, so to speak, the infinity of space and the infinity of time. Space and time were the limits within which man lived his life and which the being of God transcended. But true as this may be in itself, we desert the way of revelation when we seek to interpret the nature of God by means of the general and philosophical notion of infinity. We may not say that the infinite is God but rather that God is the infinite. That is to say, we derive our understanding of infinity from the revealed nature of God as the loving in freedom, rather than our understanding of God from the general idea of infinity. And when we do this we perceive that space and time are related differently to the being of God thus understood; that whereas His omnipresence is specially aligned with His love, His eternity makes explicit the freedom in that love. So we

[1] p. 523

arrive at the conception of time as "the form of the creation by which it happens that the creation is fitted to become the arena of the acts of His freedom".[1] In order that God may act externally in freedom, there is need of time as a form of the creation.

It is, moreover, perilous to ply our thought with the concept of infinity as such. In itself, this concept denotes a negative. It speaks of a God who is not, as we are, limited by space and time. We are finite and not infinite, and that means that we are limited in an infinite way. But in saying this have we really said anything about God? In looking at ourselves have we really reached God? Have we not rather made God an immense extension of ourselves? Have we not simply removed the limits that confine us and called the resultant God? Furthermore, if the finite is limited by the infinite, is not the reverse also true? If we are, so to speak, drops in the ocean of the infinite, must we not say that the ocean could not be apart from the drops?[2]

The omnipresence of God, since it is the omnipresence of His free love, does not exclude but specifically includes a *special* presence from which alone it can be known, and indeed from which alone it operates. God is not everywhere in the sense in which we might say that the ether is everywhere. God is everywhere as *the free subject*. That is to say, His general presence in the world can only be known from that spot where He manifests Himself as He who *gives* Himself; that is, from His Word, from Jesus Christ. In Jesus Christ as the eternal Son of God, God is present to Himself, and therefore His general presence to the world is for ever bound to His special presence in Jesus Christ.[3]

(b) Permanence and Omnipotence

In all our speech of God's oneness and of His omnipresence we have by implication spoken of His permanence and of His almightiness. But these attributes, or perfections, call now for special attention. Holding fast to the revealed truth that God is love, we are driven to the consideration of His permanence as an attribute of the freedom of His love, and to His almightiness as an attribute of His love in that freedom.

[1] p. 523   [2] pp. 523 ff.   [3] pp. 537 ff.

In speaking of permanence, we mean that God remains who He is, namely, the free subject, that He will ever affirm and establish Himself as such, that in all His ways and works He is and ever will be this.[1]

Barth prefers the word permanence to unchangeableness in this connection, for the latter word is highly misleading as applied to God and has often led theology astray. We may, indeed, say that God is in a very real and true sense unchangeable, but we may not turn the sentence round and say that the unchangeable is God. For unchangeableness, as such, means immobility and indeed death.[2] God as the living God is not the immobile and He is not the unmoved; rather is He the self-moved and only so is He the living God. He moves in that He sets up a reality other than Himself in the work of creation. He moves also in that He turns towards His creation in reconciliation and in the promise of future redemption. Furthermore He gives Himself to be moved in the prayer which He permits and indeed enjoins. But in all this He in no way ceases to be Himself, nor does He suffer any diminution of His being or receive any addition thereto. In all this He continually affirms and establishes Himself, the Self which would be no other than it is were there no existence but His own. Within Himself is the fullness of life and being, and inasmuch as this fullness is that of a free subject, He can and does cause it to overflow beyond Himself. Paradoxically enough, to all appearance, the great affirmation of the permanence of God is made in the act in which in Jesus Christ He becomes one with the creature. That the creator should Himself become creature would seem to involve a change so radical that the permanence of God could no longer be spoken of. The very opposite is however true. In Himself becoming creature, God demonstrates in the most conclusive way that in setting up an existence other than His own, the existence of the creature, He is in no way ceasing to be what He was before or becoming something other than what He was before, but is living His own free life. The life of the creature belongs absolutely to Him: He in His freedom is its absolute Lord. What then can hinder Him from living that life? When once we have got rid

[1] p. 552   [2] p. 557

of the abstract idea of unchangeableness as applied to God, an idea that can only serve to designate immobility and death, and put in its place the true idea of the one free living God who, in that He is such, has a history and indeed is a history, and who in that history remains that same one free living God whose being and nature is love, we perceive that there is no contradiction between the unchangeableness of God now rightly understood, and His moving and acting towards and within the created order.

How necessary it is to get this right understanding becomes specially apparent as we pass to the consideration of God's almightiness.[1] The term "almightiness" as applied to God designates the positive content of that freedom in which God lives His own life and in which He relates Himself to every existence outside Himself. That content is love, it is not bare power. It is God the Father who eternally loves His only begotten Son in the Holy Spirit who is the almighty; it is not the almighty, merely as such, that is God. We shall radically misconceive the almightiness of God if we start from the idea of bare power. Power simply in itself is evil. It means an overpowering, a coercing, an enchaining. If God were Almighty in the sense that He were an infinite extension of bare power, what would He be but a tyrant and a demon? Thus, to understand the almightiness of God aright certain preliminary considerations are necessary.

First, we must bear in mind that God's power is never a purely physical power. It is, above all, the power of authority, the power that has the right to rule. It is moral-juristic, *potestas*, not simply *potentia*. "What God can do *de facto* He can do *de jure*, and He can do nothing *de facto* which He cannot do *de jure*."[2] We must, of course, also say that what He can do *de jure* He can do *de facto*. But, first, we must be clear that the power of God is, above all, the power of authority, the power of right. Secondly, we must be clear that the statement about God's power must ever be made with our eyes fixed on the power which God has manifested in His revelation of Himself, but that even so, His power is not exhausted in this revelation. That is to say, the power of God does not pass over into what

[1] p. 587   [2] p. 591

He has done but remains for ever the power in which He maintains His own existence as free and absolute Lord.[1]

Further, the power of God is power of a definite kind, power which has a content. It is not just capability which could be turned in this direction or that, power that could be simply applied to any conceivable end. It is power which possesses feature, nature, quality; filled and not empty power. Its specific nature and quality is that God is able to live out of Himself: He requires nothing which is outside of Himself to be and to remain God. The power by which God lives His own life is the measure and the limit of all the powers that be. The all-power of God does not exclude other powers than His own. It is not, so to speak, the sum of all the powers that be. In setting up existences other than His own, in setting up a created world He permits the existence of other powers; but these powers move in a sphere which is determined for them by those decisions and determinations which make up God's own life and being.[2]

The point is of such capital importance that we must do all we can to clarify it. The tendency lies near, is indeed almost irresistible, to think of such things as possibility and impossibility, being and non-being, right and wrong, good and evil, as if they belonged to a realm of their own, and existed independently of the decision and determination of God. In that way they become powers to which even the life of God is subject. But there are no realms of existence or even of non-existence which are not constituted as such by those determinations in which God maintains His own life as free subject. It is in and through those determinations that the possible is constituted as the possible, the impossible as the impossible, and so on. There is nothing impossible *in abstracto*, nothing which is impossible merely as such; but there is a realm of the impossible which arises from the fact that God is a life and a history which affirms and establishes itself in perpetual act and decision. The very impossibility of twice times two making anything but four is not impossibility merely in itself; it arises from the fact that God has made it impossible, not, indeed, through some arbitrary fiat and as if the situation could have been different

[1] p. 593   [2] pp. 598 f.

but through those personal workings of the divine mind and those personal workings of the divine will which constitute the divine life and history and which are the ground of all truth and knowledge. The difficulty here disappears when once we have got rid of the idea that there is a realm of possibility and impossibility existing in its own right. There is no such realm. Apart from the self-determination of God's own being and life, there is nothing which could be conceived at all. We may not say that God *could* have decided differently, for, apart from that which He in fact *has* decided, there is just nothing whatever.

We may now pass on to describe more positively the nature of the Almighty power of God. It is the power of His knowing and of His willing.[1] God knows all: that is to say, His knowing is not determined by anything outside of Himself, as if He were dependent on that which is outside for His knowledge. Rather is it that all which exists outside of Himself is there through His knowing of it. That means that what He knows He wills, and what He wills He knows. There is nothing which is not, in the way appropriate to it, known and willed by God. We emphasize, *in the way appropriate to it*. God knows and wills the good as good, the evil as evil, the possible as possible, the impossible as impossible, and so forth. That does not mean, of course, that God is the author of evil, but that in the knowing and willing of God the evil is constituted and determined as evil. Evil could not be, nothing at all could be, apart from the divine knowing and the divine willing. Everything that may be known and willed is directly related in its own special manner to the knowing and willing of God.

We have therefore to speak of a divine fore-knowledge and a divine pre-ordination. But we must be careful not to interpret the terms "fore" and "pre" in temporal terms, as if the foreknowledge and pre-ordination of God were the temporal causes of the events which arise in time.[2] They are not such causes. How were a temporal order possible, an order different from that of God's own life and being, if it did not possess a relative independence of its own, and so an immanent law of causation? This law of causation belongs, of course, to the ordination

[1] pp. 610 ff.   [2] pp. 628 ff.

of God, and its maintenance is His own perpetual act. Nevertheless, it exists as His *creation*, as therefore different from Himself, so that within its sphere there is an ordering other than the ordering of God's own life and being. The fore-knowledge and pre-ordination are therefore not to be understood temporally. They indicate the difference and superiority of the knowing and willing of God with regard to all temporal knowing and willing. They signify that God's knowing and willing is not dependent upon events as they arise in the temporal order, but that this temporal order can only exist because behind it and over it there is a divine mind and a divine will. Because God knows, there is such a thing as human knowing, and because He wills there is such a thing as human willing.

(c) *Eternity and Glory*

The treatment of the divine attributes is concluded with a consideration of God's eternity and God's glory. The former is specially related to the divine freedom, and the latter to the love in that freedom.

We shall not apprehend the eternity of God aright if we think of it as the infinite prolongation of time. What would that have to do with God?[1] But neither must we regard it as time's negation. Once more what would a negative have to do with God?[2] Rather must we say that God's eternity is the principle of all time. By that we mean that the distinctions of beginning, continuance, and end, which belong to time in our experience, are grounded in the decisions and self-determinations wherein God lives His own life as God. They do not condition the life of God; the life of God conditions them. Because God lives His life as pure decision, pure determination, pure subject, beginning, continuance, and end are not separate in Him but united. He "is" pure beginning, pure continuance, pure end. Thus He is eternal, and His eternity includes time and flows over into time constituting beginning, continuance, and end in time.[3] That which is peculiar to the history of man is that it is conditioned by time. Without time man can originate nothing, continue nothing, bring nothing to an end. That which is peculiar to the history of God is that it conditions time.

[1] p. 686   [2] p. 688   [3] p. 689

Without God's life, God's decisions, God's acts, there can be no time.

We shall, therefore, think most truly of God's eternity when we consider it as pre-temporalness, super-temporalness, and post-temporalness.[1] God is pre-temporal. We had better interpret that quite literally and even in a physical sense. God was there before we were, before all things. That may sound trivial and unmeaning. It is however highly important and full of meaning. God does not depend on the creation; does not depend on anything other than Himself for the fullness of His own life. There was no lack in Him which had to be made good by any creature. On the contrary, it was out of the fullness of His own life and love that the creation arose through His own free act.[2]

God is super-temporal. By this we mean that He stands in a positive relation to all the sequence of time. He is no less God, the Lord over time, than He was at time's beginning and will be at time's ending. God's eternity accompanies time as it takes its course. It stands over time as the horizon stands over the revolving earth.[3]

God is post-temporal. This sentence emphasizes that time has a goal; that it is not in itself eternity; that time which does not lead to God's eternity leads to sheer nothingness. Time has not its goal immanent in itself. The goal is set to it, is determined for it, by the decision of God.[4]

We touch here the problem of eschatology which bulks so largely in our modern theological thought, and which has received new significance from recent New Testament criticism. It is important therefore to remind ourselves that there should be no thought of competition between the concepts of God's pre-temporalness, super-temporalness and post-temporalness. In Reformation times there was a tendency to emphasize the first of these to the neglect of the others. All that happened in time was referred to the eternal decrees and counsels of God before time began. The result was that a certain hopelessness and joylessness came into life, a feeling that all had already happened, and that no new activity of God was to be expected. Later on, the emphasis was shifted to God's super-temporalness.

[1] p. 698   [2] p. 700   [3] pp. 702 ff.   [4] pp. 709 ff.

God was the eternal, accompanying and penetrating all time. Man was made attentive to his present and positive possibilities. A certain activism which resulted in a secularization of life came to rule. The present was emphasized to the exclusion of the past and the future. Thus, God Himself as subject was lost sight of in the evolution of mere happening. Man sought for absolute values within the flow of time and history.

To-day the tendency is widespread to overstress the post-temporalness of God; to relate time to its end, its *eschaton*; to forget that He who will be is also He who was and He who is. The result of this has been twofold. On the one hand, there has arisen in certain circles a one-sided other-worldliness, a tendency to withdraw from temporal concerns as from things without essential meaning. On the other hand, there has been a resurgence of that secularity formerly associated with the idea of God's super-temporalness. The ideas of crisis and judgment have been imported into temporal movements. There is much of the eschatological temper in modern socialism and communism and revolution-movements generally. Since eschatology in its primitive forms has been perceived to be untenable, it has been transformed into a kind of mysticism of history which has led to secularism.[1]

All these errors and injuries can be avoided only as it is recognized that God is eternal as pure beginning, pure continuance, and pure end; that His pre-temporalness, super-temporalness, and post-temporalness are of equal truth and significance; that the God who concerns us now is the God who was before we were, and will be when our temporal life shall have come to an end; that our times are in His eternal hands; and, above all, that eternity is God Himself and God Himself eternity. This last point is of decisive importance. Eternity is no mere qualification of the being of God; it is God Himself in the free determination of His life as pure subject.

We cannot speak aright of God's eternity unless we pass at once to speak of His Majesty and Glory. One might speak of an eternal "being" without conveying any suggestion of splendour. There is no splendour in mere abstract being.[2] But God is not abstract "being", and His eternity is not the duration of being

[1] pp. 711 ff.   [2] p. 722

68

as such. God is free subject, and to his eternal being belongs Lordship. He is, therefore, in Himself majestic and glorious. And in that He is glorious He has the power not only to assert His Lordship as a kind of brute fact, but, as it were, to demonstrate Himself, to make Himself known as He is in Himself, and to create a recognition which answers to this self-demonstration; a recognition such as will be accompanied by joy, longing, and satisfaction.

The concept which lies nearest to our hand for the designation of the glory of God is that of beauty.[1] We may say that God is infinitely beautiful, the ground and norm of all beauty. But we shall say this with circumspection. We shall be careful to avoid all mere aestheticism in speaking of God, and we shall give no support to the idea that the knowledge of God is reached by way of aesthetic intuition. Aestheticism in this realm is as definitely to be called in question as intellectualism and voluntarism.[2] God is not, so to speak, an aesthetic magnitude. Nevertheless, it would be no true apprehension of God which did not convey a sense of beauty. Beauty is not one of the attributes of God, as grace, holiness, mercy and so forth are attributes; it is the form in which these attributes reach us. We use the concept of beauty to indicate that the glory of God is something worthy of our love. Our thankfulness for God's revelation of Himself as grace is not a mere relief that our punishment is averted and our life established; it is a gladness which reflects and echoes something of the fullness of the life of God Himself. And our obedience is not simply a duty which we recognize as owed to one who has a right to it; it is the sonship which the eternal sonship in God Himself makes to echo within the sphere of human life. Thus, we may speak not simply of the glory of God, but of a glorifying of God from our side.[3] Not that we are capable, of ourselves, of being the echo of God's glory, and so of glorifying Him; but, in that God exhibits and demonstrates His own eternal life and being within the sphere of our creaturely life, He reflects and echoes His glory within our thanks and our obedience. The glory of God is the glory of His eternal love.

As one ponders over the exposition which Barth presents of

[1] p. 733   [2] p. 735   [3] p. 753

the divine attributes and their mutual connections, an exposition of which we have been able to give the merest indication, one cannot but feel that, without setting out with any apologetic intentions, Barth has in fact accomplished a powerful work of apologetic. He has indirectly but most effectually demolished the objection that the Biblical doctrine of God is a mere piece of anthropomorphism. A God who was simply decked out with such qualities as grace, mercy, righteousness, and the like, or who was equipped with such powers as omnipotence, omnipresence, and so forth, might easily be dismissed as the product of man's anthropomorphic tendencies. But, in that case, the content of these qualities and powers would have been derived from general ideas. A general idea of love and of power would have been taken up and applied to God. No anthropomorphic conception of God shows any trace of concern about the *subject* of the attributes which are assigned to Him. The subject disappears in the attributes. He is a mere deification of the attributes. He is a mere peg on which to hang the attributes. The process of anthropomorphism proceeds and must proceed, naïvely or subtly, as follows: there are, let us say, goodness in man and power in the world; and so we posit an infinite extension of these, and call the resultant God. The content of the word God is derived from the attributes assigned to Him. But Barth has shown that the God of whom the Bible speaks is no deification of attributes whose content is derived from general ideas. With this God, it is throughout the subject which gives the content to the attributes, and not the attributes to the subject. We learn what God's love and power are, not from general ideas of love and power, but entirely from the witness given to the action of God in revelation. No anthropomorphism proceeds in this fashion. All anthropomorphism is unmasked as such in the doctrine here put forward. Barth has supplied a proof of the reality of God before which any so-called proof attempted along the lines of ordinary apologetic pales. We may find here a confirmation of the conviction which dominates all Barth's thought: that true theological thinking, thinking which remains bound to its object really achieves its goal. It brings out into clear view the reality of the object from which it starts and which governs its course.

CHAPTER IV

THE DOCTRINE OF GOD (3)

God's Election of Grace

THE first part of Barth's doctrine of God with which we have
hitherto been concerned is an endeavour to set forth the being
and life which God has in Himself, as that being and life appear
in the Biblical witness to revelation. But the Christian doctrine
of God is not brought to an end in the consideration of God
merely in Himself. If it be true that in Jesus dwelt all the
fullness of the Godhead bodily, God cannot be known apart
from that relationship in which He stands to men in Jesus
Christ. He cannot be known apart from this, for He "is" not
apart from this. Certainly man himself is no part of the being
and reality of God. But the reality of the relationship itself,
the eternal decision in which God in His love and freedom binds
Himself to man, can be thought of in no way as apart from
God's own being. We cannot go back behind that decision to
find a God merely in Himself, for behind that decision there
is no God to be found.

We are accordingly confronted with God's choice or election
of man for fellowship with Himself, and the doctrine of this
choice is a substantive part of the doctrine of God.

We must begin by reiterating our thesis that Jesus Christ is
the source and goal of all our knowledge of God. Not the source
only, as if there were given in Him a mere impetus, so that we
could now go on our own way; and not the mere continuation,
as if the knowledge of God in Christ were but an advancement
of the knowledge which we had gained in some other way.[1]
In Jesus Christ, God announces Himself over against all our
imaginations and errors. Jesus Christ is the overflowing to us
of the life of God in all the fullness of its love and freedom, so
that we should not be speaking of God at all were we not
speaking of this fullness. We advance in our knowledge of God

[1] *Dog.*, II, 1, p. 2

71

from faith to faith. And the object of our faith is ever the same: the God who gives Himself to us as grace in Jesus Christ.

Since, therefore, Jesus Christ is Himself the reality of the relationship which God establishes with man, since he is God's turning towards man, we can understand our election in no other way than as an election of grace.[1] But, before we address ourselves to the consideration of what this means, we must let our thought rest on the fact that it is verily election, choice. We have to do with a free decision of God not to satisfy Himself with the fullness of His own independent life, but to allow that fullness to flow out towards beings other than Himself.[2] Because He is the loving in freedom, He could do this; and in His love and freedom He has done it. But He *need* not do it. There is nothing which could necessitate such an action; it is free sovereign decision. This decision is not conditioned by anything outside of God which might claim it or merit it. Nor is it conditioned by anything in God's own nature which would make it necessary for Him to enter into fellowship with beings other than Himself, for He already has the fullness of fellowship within His own being. Since, however, God lives not only in Himself and for Himself but for man, that fact can only be referred to an eternal divine decision in which He determines His own life and being, not only inwardly but outwardly. We need, therefore, to put full weight on the two words, "choice" and "grace", to describe the nature of the relationship which God establishes with man in Jesus Christ.

In all the great classic expositions of the doctrine of election or predestination, emphasis has been laid on three things: the freedom, the mystery, and the righteousness of the electing will of God. This emphasis is rightful and must be preserved. But—and here the classic theories almost without exception fall short—the emphasis must be made in the light of the fact that this electing will is a will of *grace*. Certainly we bow before a mystery when we speak of election; a mystery which awes us into silence. But this silence is not a silence of helplessness before some capricious will. It is a silence of adoration induced by our recognition that our election is verily an election of grace; something, that is, that results from no necessity on the

[1] p. 8   [2] p. 9

part of God, and from no merit on our part, but which has its
ground in God's good pleasure alone. And, when we speak of
the righteousness of the divine election and predestination, our
confession of this righteousness is not something which we
make in the dark, as if we were in no position to see how
righteous this divine election was. On the contrary, we behold
this righteousness. We perceive that God in His election does
that which is worthy of Him; does that which corresponds
with His nature.[1]

It becomes evident that we are confronted at the outset with
the necessity of departing in a certain radical fashion from the
traditional conceptions of election. Barth cannot refrain from
expressing amazement that all the great exponents of the
predestination doctrine failed to perceive its true connection
with Christology. How was it that they did not see that Jesus
Christ, in whom God turns Himself to man, is one with the
electing will of God? How was it that in their search for the
ground of the divine election they actually strove to go behind
Christ to some *decretum absolutum* (absolute decree) in the
inscrutable will of God?[2] What do we know, what can we know,
of the will of God for man unless we perceive it in Jesus Christ?
If the will of God, which is identical with the reality of Jesus
Christ, is not, after all, the real, final, and ultimate will of God;
if there be some hidden decree lying behind the decision of
God to move outwards to man in Christ, does not revelation
cease to be revelation? If Jesus Christ be merely the instrument
of the will of God, merely the means by which men are either
chosen or rejected, according to some inscrutable decree which
is not identical with the reality of His person and work, then
there is but an arbitrary connection between the real will of
God and Him. It is necessary in this matter to depart from
Augustine, and more decisively still from Calvin. Jesus Christ
is not a mere instrument of the divine election. He is the
subject of election; the chosen one in the midst of humanity;
the effectuation of God's choice of man for Himself, and of
Himself for man. Men are not chosen simply through Him,
but *in* Him and *for* Him. The root of every error that has
crept into the predestination doctrine—and how calamitous

[1] pp. 28.ff.   [2] pp. 70 ff.

the errors have been—lies in the unaccountable blindness of its classic exponents to the fact, which stands out with crystal clearness in the Biblical witness, that the ground of the electing will of God is identical with the reality of Jesus Christ.

Barth will not deny that there is an exegetical problem to be faced here. There are some scriptural passages which speak of the divine election without direct reference to its ground in Jesus Christ. But how came it to pass that the great exponents of the doctrine here forsook the fundamental principle on which, in other matters, they were so insistent that the key to the Scriptures is Christ? How came it to pass that they perceived with such clearness that all Biblical teaching on such themes as justification, reconciliation, regeneration, sanctification, and redemption, must be interpreted in the light of Christ; that they could so rightfully insist that Christ Himself was man's justification, reconciliation, regeneration, sanctification and redemption; but that, when they came to deal with the most fundamental theme of all, the divine election, they could seek its ground outside Christ and behind Christ in some *decretum absolutum*?[1] And, surprisingly enough, not only did the protagonists of the election doctrine fall into this error, but those who opposed them never perceived where the root of the error lay. "The doctrine of God's election of grace is the sum of the gospel."[2] All that makes the gospel truly gospel, good news, is summed up in it. But the tragedy has been that this mighty and glorious theme has been treated as if it were something other than gospel; as if it were a kind of dark patch lying behind the gospel and extinguishing its light.

The divine election of grace means that God in the eternal counsel of His will has chosen for Himself fellowship with man; and for man fellowship with Himself—thus a double choice and predestination. This double choice is revealed in Jesus Christ and takes effect on the stage of time in Him. Jesus Christ is both the electing God and the elected man.[3] He is the electing God, the will of God turned outwards towards man. As the eternal Son of the Father, He is very God. His will is one with God's will. There is no other will of God for man

---

[1] p. 166   [2] p. 9   [3] pp. 101 ff.

but that which is expressed, realized and fulfilled in Him. And Jesus Christ is also the elected man. In Him our humanity is laid hold of and gathered into the life of God. Jesus Christ was true man. In the light of Jesus Christ we can no longer speak of God purely in Himself, or of man purely in himself. We can only speak of God and man united in that communion wherein God meets man in pure sovereign grace, and man meets God in faith and obedience. In the beginning—not in God's beginning, for God, as we have already seen, has no beginning, He is Himself pure beginning of all things—God binds Himself to man and man to Himself. The pre-existent God-man who enters the sphere of time in Jesus Christ is Himself the reality of the divine decree. It is not, of course, as if our humanity existed eternally in God as part of His being. It exists eternally in God as object of His choice, of His free grace, of the over-flowing of that love wherein God is God.

And now we have to take a further step: to say that God chooses is also to say that He rejects. He chooses to be man's God, and He chooses not to be not man's God. This negative decision is just as truly a decision as the positive. Man is not left to himself. He does not fall outside of that choice when He refuses the election of grace, for, outside of that choice, there is nothing to fall into.

The man to whom God binds Himself is the man in sin and fall. Even as creature man is *homo labilis*, man liable to fall; in his actual existence he is *homo lapsus*, man fallen, man who seeks to isolate himself over against God and to make himself his own God. Therefore, as such, he lies under the divine rejection. But the election of grace, eternal in the counsels of God, is not nullified by man's sin and fall. In Jesus Christ, God takes upon Himself the sentence of rejection and bears it in man's stead. In Jesus Christ, God Himself enters into the dark shadow of man's rejection and dissipates it. Christ's Cross signalizes God's absolute condemnation of man; His Resurrection, God's acquittal and justification. The former still remains in force, but only as the reverse side of the latter.[1] There is, therefore, because of Jesus Christ no positive decision of God to reject man, but only the gracious decision to accept

[1] pp. 175 ff.

75

him; that is to say, there are not two spheres, one of election and the other of reprobation, standing independently over against each other. The negative decision of reprobation is reprobation only of the man who refuses the election of grace, who attempts to isolate himself from it. Man can do this by virtue of his natural freedom, a freedom which election in no way annuls, but rather which it presupposes. But the point to emphasize is that man does not stand on some neutral ground from which he can, purely out of himself, accept or refuse the grace of God. He is taken off all neutral ground and set by God in the crisis of decision. Precisely in that crisis his freedom truly emerges, and that crisis it is, and not man's independent choice, which determines whether his response will be faith or unfaith, obedience or disobedience.

And now, in following the direction of Holy Scripture, we are faced by the fact that the first reference of the divine election is not to man in general and not to the individual man, but to a chosen community, named Israel in the Old Testament, and the Church in the New. Jesus Christ is the Saviour of all men because He is first and foremost the Messiah of Israel and the Lord of the Church. But here a word of caution is necessary. It is not as if there were an election of the community which might be thought of as in some sense independent of the election of the individual man; as if the community were some sort of mystical magnitude which itself determined the salvation of the individual man. Such an idea "is the result of Jewish or clerical phantasy and arrogance".[1]

It cannot be too strongly emphasized that it is the individual man who is the object of the divine election and not the community as such. There are no elect nations, classes or communities, simply in themselves.[2] Both Israel and the Church exist to serve the electing purpose of God, which is for the individual man. They form, so to speak, the space surrounding Jesus Christ; the spot from which He, as the electing God and the elected man, operate in the world.[3] And they do this because in their life and history they mirror and reflect the great divine events of election and rejection which took place in Him, and so bear witness to Him and mediate Him to the

[1] p. 216   [2] p. 349   [3] p. 217

76

world. The peculiar function of Israel in this regard is to mirror and illustrate the divine rejection which became event in the crucifixion of the Son of God, and so of the world which passes away in Him; the peculiar function of the Church, the divine election which was manifested in His resurrection, and so the new coming world of God.[1] Neither this rejection nor this election are more than mirrored, more than witnessed to, by Israel and the Church. The history of Israel and of the Church are not in themselves the divine rejection and election. But, inasmuch as Christ is Himself the meaning and substance of the life of Israel and of the Church, so that only in Him and for Him have they a place of their own in the divine ordering, they point in their history to His Cross and Resurrection which signalize man's rejection in his sinful actuality, a rejection which is the reverse side of his election through God's will of grace. These two historical magnitudes, Israel and the Church, are therefore fundamentally one and the same. "The one community of God has in its form as Israel to serve the setting forth of the divine judgment, in its form as Church the setting forth of the divine mercy. To the one community of God is given, there (in Israel) its departing form; here (in the Church), its coming form."[2]

We shall not say that the actual Israel was the direct object of the divine rejection, and that the actual Church is the direct object of the divine election. That would attribute to each an independent election of its own and quite apart from the election in Christ. It would also presuppose a predetermination of God for rejection existing quite independently of His election of grace. But the history of Israel mirrors and expresses the sinful actuality of all mankind, and so the divine rejection; while the Church bears witness to the new humanity in Christ, and so to the divine election. Both Israel and the Church point to the divine promise which is fulfilled in Christ. And therefore they are, so to speak, the space round Christ, the sphere in which He as the electing God and the elected man are witnessed, and in which He functions in the world.

One further observation is necessary at this point. Our thought must dwell upon the fact that the election of grace is a

[1] pp. 219 ff.   [2] p. 215

living, moving thing. We shall radically misconceive election
and predestination if we think of it, as the old exponents of the
doctrine so largely did, as a mere stationary decree fixing in
advance all that should follow after.[1] That would make it a
dead thing, a fate; or a mere first cause; or a driving and im-
pelling force. It would empty history of all actuality and make
it a kind of cinematograph reel in which nothing really
happened. What we have to do with is no dead decree, but the
action of the living, electing God, upon the acts and decisions
of men; an action in which these acts and decisions are determined in one way or another but determined as *acts* and
decisions, that is, as expressions of freedom. The difficulty here
largely disappears when we realize that God is Himself a history
interpenetrating the history of man. His eternal decision, which
is nothing less than Himself in action, bears down, as it were, on
human life and history: bringing it continually to crisis, and
so constituting the inner core of history generally and the
history of the individual man. Predestination is salvation
history, and, as such, the secret of all history. The election
decree is a self-determining of God's own life, and so it cannot
be isolated from His presence and action within the life of man.

We may now proceed to the consideration of the election of
the individual man. We have already noted that it is not any
community or collectivity, as such, which is the real object of
the divine election: but man as an individual, the single man,
man in his simple humanness, we might say. Certainly this
individual man stands in a multitude of relations to the various
forms of collectivity in which he lives his life. Nevertheless,
it is to him in his individuality, in his self-hood, that the word
of God is addressed; and it is in him as an individuality that the
election of God takes place. No collectivity can be addressed
as "thou"; only the individual can be the subject of direct
address.

But what do we mean by individuality from the standpoint
of the divine election? What is the nature of this individuality
as it is confronted with the electing purpose of God? We must
take our point of departure from the fact that the individual,
as we know him, is a sinner; that his individuality as an

[1] p. 202

actuality in the world is a sinful individuality, and so an impossibility in the sight of God. That is to say, he is the man who strives continually to isolate himself as over against God and to make himself his own God. Instead of receiving his individuality as a gift of God, something therefore which attains its true nature only as it becomes a response to grace, he stands upon it and claims it as his own.[1] Now, the Word of God announces that this cannot be done; and, in point of fact, the individual as an isolated entity readily falls a victim to some authoritarianism or totalitarianism or other.[2] The actual individual, therefore, stands under the rejection of God, and must cease to be. But he ceases to be in order that the true individual, the elect man, may appear. He stands under the judgment of Christ's death, a judgment borne by Christ in His death on man's behalf, in order that he may receive the promise of his true manhood in Christ's resurrection.

And now we have to say that the individual man in hearing and believing the promise, and in thus becoming the elect man, receives a special designation which marks him off from those who do not hear and believe.[3] His election, that is, cannot remain hidden from himself or from others. But, in saying this, we must be careful to guard ourselves against misunderstanding. We do not mean that the elect man is designated as such though certain virtues and qualities stamped upon him, which he or others, looking upon objectively, might perceive as the proof of his election. His election does not yield itself to mere inspection. It is not something which could be deduced from any such objective examination. But it directly witnesses itself both to the man himself and to others in the course which his life takes. Because there is that in him and about him which transcends his own nature and qualities as such, it will assert itself in the actual living of his life as an elect man. Only as his election fulfils itself in his life can it be known to himself or to others. To gather the matter up in a sentence: the man must not stop in order to look at himself and try to assure himself that what he finds there is evidence of his election; he must simply go on his way believing in the *promise*. In believing in the promise he will *be* the elect man; and in believing in the promise will he know himself and be known by others as such.

The election of the individual man is, in reality, a derivation from the election of Jesus Christ.[1] The individual man recognizes his own election in that of Jesus Christ. As his life becomes a hearing and receiving of the promise which is his in the election of Jesus Christ, that election becomes the transcendent mystery of his own existence. It stamps him as the true individual, and sets him apart from the rest of men. It makes him himself and not just one of a mass or number. His ordinary, actual, individuality, inasmuch as it is sinful, and so lies under the rejection of God, has in itself no truth and significance. It cannot witness to the truth of God. For this reason, it is continually threatened by some authoritarianism or other. And yet just that fact about it, just the fact that, in itself, individuality as we commonly know it possesses no truth or significance, has for ever been abolished in the election of Christ. In Christ, man's individuality, man's singleness, the fact that man is no mere part of some worldly collectivity, the fact that individuality is an elect thing, is grounded in the eternal counsels of God.

When we enquire what is the peculiar designation of the elected individual, how is his life determined by God's election of grace, what course does it follow, to what end is it led, we are first met in Scripture with the answer: the elect man is such in that he allows himself to be loved by God. "That is the determination of Jesus Christ Himself, to be in our flesh the man loved from eternity and for eternity by God. That is the determination of Israel and the Church: they are the people and the assembly of those who are loved by God in Jesus Christ."[2] And the single individual man can be no other and can wish for nothing greater than to be loved by God with this eternal love, this love which does not stop at the boundaries of creaturehood, but which, in and through God's own decision, overflows those boundaries. When we say that the elect man allows himself to be loved by God, we mean that he sets aside all claims of his own to that love; that he permits a love which he has not in any way earned, not in any way deserved, to

[1] p. 387   [2] p. 455

determine his life. He does not try to stretch himself beyond his creaturehood, and he in no way seeks to evade the judgment passed upon him as a sinner. He quite simply allows God's love to overflow to him, and finds in that love his one sure ground of hope.

Thus he knows himself to be determined for blessedness.[1] And so, in his daily living, he goes forward with a joy in his heart which is a ray or drop of the joy of God in the creature whom He has chosen for fellowship with Himself, and thus of the joy wherein God lives His own life. And that means that this joy will take the form of thankfulness. What has he to bring to God but his thanks? His thanks is the human correspondence with the blessedness for which he is determined. It is this blessedness accepted, rejoiced in, and referred to its eternal ground in the divine election of grace.[2]

But there is something further to be said which is of decisive moment. This love of God overflowing to man, this blessedness determined for him as his end and goal, must not come to an end in his receiving of them. Man is not simply the object of God's love and blessedness; he is also the subject of them. That is to say, he does not just passively receive; he actively shares. And that means that this love and blessedness must pass beyond himself in the direction of the world which God in His election of grace has chosen for His own. By this love and blessedness the elect man is determined as witness of God's election to others.[3] The individual, in being elected, becomes a further stage along which God's election of grace takes effect in the world. It cannot be his thought that those others whom the Word of God has not yet reached belong to the rejected; or that they may be divided into two classes, those destined for election and those for rejection. In his own life he has come to know that in himself he is rejected, but in Christ he is accepted. How, then, can he look upon any man as simply rejected? He must bear witness to the election of grace, which is valid even in the sphere of rejection. And this he will do, not as something special and additional to the ordinary tasks of his life, but in the very living of his life as an elected man.

We conclude the exposition of the doctrine of election with

[1] p. 455   [2] p. 456   [3] p. 457

a brief note on the rejected man, the content of his life and the way in which that life is determined. We have had, by now, ample opportunity to reflect on the fact that rejection is but the reverse side of election. It is none the less real on that account. Election would not be election, it would not be a real choice, unless rejection were veritably rejection; unless it had its ground in the divine will. The rejected man is the man who isolates himself over against God's grace; the man who, in the crisis into which God's election of grace places him, sets himself in opposition thereto. "God is for him, but he is against God. . . . God lays hold of him, but he withdraws himself from God. God forgives his sins, but he repeats them as if they were not forgiven. God frees him from the guilt and punishment of his fall, but he lives on as the prisoner of Satan."[1]

In dealing with the predestination of the rejected man, we must recognize that we have to do with the will of God in a sense quite different from that in the case of the predestination of the elect. We might call this will rather a "not willing", so long as we recognize that this not willing is not an absence of willing, not a withdrawing, not a passive thing, but, after its manner, as much an exercise of the divine will as in the election of grace.[2] By designating it as a "not willing", we mean that it does not exist independently of God's will to elect. The rejected man exists as the object of God's not willing; that is to say, his existence is determined by the fact that God will not have him as he is. He exists as rejected in so far as he attempts to live in withdrawal from that positive will of God which claims him for the election of grace. His life can be no real life. It is a life without meaning and substance, and without a future. It can only run to ground upon itself. And it is such a life because it is determined as such by the will of God, which, in electing him for grace, condemns him as one who strives to live in independence of grace. The content of the life of the rejected man can, therefore, only be seen from the point of view of election. It has no independent content of its own. It is not in reality a self-determined life, which would at least give it some positive significance; for all men, whether they know it or not, whether they will have it so or not, live under

[1] p. 498   [2] p. 499

82

the predetermining decision of God, which rejects and condemns all the isolation of man as over against Him because it chooses fellowship between man and Himself.

Inasmuch, therefore, as the rejected life is, in the form appropriate to it, a God-determined life, it performs a service, though of a negative kind, to the election of grace. We may describe this service briefly as follows. First, the rejected life is so determined as to make visible the subject addressed by the gospel.[1] It represents the world as it stands in need of redemption. Without the rejected man, the special office and commission of the elect to witness to the free grace of God in the world could not be exercised. Without him, and, we may add, without his presence in the elected man himself—for the elected man stands continually under the threat of rejection, a rejection which is only removed in the election of Jesus Christ on his behalf—grace would be forgotten as grace.

Further, the rejected man makes and keeps visible that isolation over against God which the electing purpose of God has stamped as deception and lie. Without this negative service which is rendered, God's truth would not become manifest in the world as truth.[2]

Once more the rejected man makes evident the purpose of the gospel, which is to assure to man a future. The rejected man, as such, has no future. His individuality possesses no eternal ground. He represents the world as it passes away, a world which is revealed as passing away in and through the election of grace. Apart from his existence, the purpose of God to give to man, who, as he is, has no future, participation in His own eternal life would not become manifest. The limit which God sets to man's life merely in itself cannot be made manifest save through the surmounting and surpassing of this limit in God's election of grace. This limit is established in the existence of the rejected man.[3]

It would be difficult to measure the service which Barth has rendered by his exposition of the doctrine of election and predestination, an exposition which we have been able to set forth only in meagre outline. The extent of this service may be long in appearing, but it cannot be indefinitely concealed. There is

[1] p. 504   [2] p. 506   [3] p. 507

probably no doctrine which has exercised such revolutionary and stabilizing power over life and society as the doctrine of election. Secular social theories have their day, and they exercise much influence. But they leave man at last defenceless against the forces of tyranny and oppression, and they involve him in a continual struggle merely to maintain an existence in which there is no real purpose. And the root reason of their failure is that they are unable to root man's individuality in any sure ground. This service was accomplished, with the imperfection and brokenness which inevitably accompany all human endeavour, by the classical exponents of the Biblical doctrine of election. Through their efforts, human individuality was seen to rest on an eternal foundation, and the tyranny of mere might and force was broken. That true individuality *might* be manifested upon the field of time and history was shown to be the goal and purpose of all temporal happening; that, as a matter of fact, this individuality *did* appear, guaranteed and guarded the existence of real and genuine society. Man, not simply the idea or ideal of humanity, but man as concrete human being, man as free and responsible subject, was shown to be rooted in eternal reality and validity. And this was accomplished, not by means of some philosophical interpretation of man's nature and constitution which could only operate as a theory, and which could scarcely do more than represent true individuality as an ideal to be pursued, but by pointing to a predetermined election of God to which all the decisions of men could only be a correspondence in one form or another.

It is difficult to see how a world which has just emerged from a gigantic struggle with a tyrannous totalitarianism, a world in which the principle of individuality has been preserved, yet so as by fire, and in which it is still precarious, can remain indefinitely indifferent to the Christian doctrine of election. What can individuality mean unless it be predetermined individuality? How can it remain valid as a mere phenomenon, a mere object in the midst of the other objects which make up the universe? Are not individuality and phenomenalism of every kind a contradiction in terms? The terrible perversions from which the old election doctrine suffered, perversions which did so much to arrest its power, are removed in Barth's exposition; and they are removed through no mere rational criticism, but from the side of revelation itself. Everything which would confound the will of God with mere caprice, everything, that is, which would confound it with mere chance or fate—and what is more a thing of chance than a capricious will—here disappears.

There is a further observation to be made. It is that the doctrine of election alone, as it stands in Barth's exposition, can secure Christology from the reproach of mythology. Mythology arises from man's projection of himself and his world into the sphere of the divine; and it is often asserted that the doctrine of the Incarnation is a signal instance of the mythologizing process. Here, it is said, is an outstanding case of a man being exalted to divine heights. Christology, it is contended, is mythology *par excellence*. And the kind of Christology which would represent the divinity of Christ as a full or exemplary expression of the divinity latent in all men must ever be exposed to the accusation of mythologizing. But the conception of the God-man, as it stands in the Biblical doctrine of election, means not the projection of the human into the divine, but the projection of the divine into the human. So far from the God-man establishing man's divinity, it decisively denies it and brings man under a radical judgment. God is manifested, not as the extension to infinity of man's being, but as the entire rejection of man in his empirical actuality. In fact, all mythologizing is unmasked as such in the conception of the God-man, and branded as idolatry. And it may very well be asked whether all human thinking which rejects the conception of the God-man can be anything but mythology at last.

CHAPTER V

THE DOCTRINE OF GOD (4)

God's Commandment and the Problem of Ethics

THE doctrine of God is concluded and completed in the consideration of the divine commandment which gathers up into itself the problem of ethics. It is impossible to treat of God's election of grace without passing on directly to deal with the question of what God demands of the man who is the object of this election. Since election is the determining of man's existence by God, the question of man's own self-determination inevitably arises: a question which covers the whole field of man's ethical behaviour. We have to note at the outset that, in dealing with this question, we do not in the least degree step outside the circle drawn by the divine election; and that means that we are still occupied with the consideration of God's own life and being. Certainly, man in himself does not belong to the doctrine of God; but Jesus, the God-man, in whom and for whom man is chosen by God, does.[1] A God without Jesus Christ would not be God at all. Accordingly the one true God, the God and Father of our Lord Jesus Christ, is the Lord of the covenant between Himself and man, the God who takes man into partnership with Himself and so into a correspondence with His own will.

We have already seen what it is that God wills *with* the elected man. He wills "to rule over him, to take him into His service, to give him the task of participation in His own work, to make Him a witness of Jesus Christ and so a witness of His own glory."[2] But, that being the case, man is clearly no thing, no neuter, but a person; and so we are driven to a special consideration of the question of what God wills *from* him, what God demands of him. That God wills to rule over man raises the question of man's obedience; that He determines him for His service means that He takes him in claim; that He becomes

[1] p. 565   [2] p. 565

his covenant partner makes Him necessarily judge over him, makes Him the law of man's existence.[1] The ruling grace which becomes operative in man's election becomes the commanding grace over man's actions and decisions. The gospel, the great indicative, becomes law and commandment; becomes the great imperative.[2] Thus, both Dogmatics and Ethics belong to the doctrine of God; and, inasmuch as Ethics designates a universal human problem, we may regard it as the sphere in which Dogmatics becomes a universal concern. The true ethic is a theological ethic.

We must not be deterred from taking up the problem of Ethics into Dogmatics by the objection that we are thus giving an illegitimate meaning to the term Ethics, a meaning other than it possesses in our ordinary thought and speech. We are free to take up concepts where we find them without binding ourselves to the meaning which they may there possess. No concept possesses an absolutely uniform signification, and certainly that of Ethics does not. Moreover, Dogmatics cannot leave any concept as it exists in our mind untested.[3] But there is no ground for not taking up the concept of Ethics into Dogmatics. And, roughly speaking, we may define the ethical question in its general signification as the question after the ground and possibility of the fact that, in the crowd and multiplicity of human actions and modes of action, there arise certain constancies, laws, rules, customs, and continuities.[4]

These laws and constancies are placed in ethical enquiry under the question of their rightfulness, suitability and worth. Ethics will not leave these things as mere facts, it will raise them as questions.

The fact that the ethical question should arise at all, and that it is in some form universal, cannot be, to the theologian, a cause for surprise; though, to the philosopher, it must constitute a problem in itself. To the theologian, however, it can be no problem, for the ethical question is actually put to man by God in His choosing of him for fellowship with Himself. God's electing grace has, as a matter of fact, placed man from all eternity under His commandment. From that choice and that commandment man derives his existence. And man exists in

[1] p. 566   [2] p. 567   [3] p. 568   [4] p. 569

that he acts. Therefore, as long as man lives and acts he cannot
extricate himself from the ethical question. It can, therefore,
be readily understood how it comes to pass that all kinds of
ethical systems should have arisen in the course of man's life.[1]

But, though the theologian can account for the rise of these
systems, he is bound to stigmatize them as inherently impossible and as the fruit of man's fall and sin. They make their
appearance because man, instead of allowing himself, through
God's grace, to be himself the answer to the ethical question;
instead, that is, of living under the commandment of God,
inevitably and without question, seeks himself to be as God and
to determine out of his own thought and decision what is good
and what is evil. So far from these ethical systems being signs
of man's inherent nobility, they are signs of His fall from God
and His grace. The ethical question is not simply put to man by
God's commandment, it is answered for him in God's election
of grace.

All independent answers from the side of man are set aside
by God's grace, and are shown to arise from an illegitimate
activity. "The grace of God protests against all ethics set up
by man as such."[2] But this grace protests not simply negatively
but positively. It protests because it puts its own answer to
the ethical question into active operation. Jesus Christ, who
fulfils the commandment of God, is Himself the answer to the
ethical question. In Him man's sanctification and taking in
claim by God becomes event.[3]

Now all this possesses all-important consequences for our
attitude to the ethical problem. We are faced with the fact
that there cannot legitimately be a general ethic existing
alongside and independently of the revealed law and commandment of God; an ethic based upon a prior examination of man's
capacities, nature and circumstances; an ethic arising out of
some world-view. General ethic is the attempt to set up the
law as if the law were not already set up in the command
which belongs to God's election of grace. It grounds the law
in man's nature and will, as if that nature and will were not
radically called in question and placed under judgment by
God's commandment. It stands, therefore, not in continuity

[1] p. 572   [2] p. 573   [3] p. 573

with, but in contradiction to, the Word of God; and this contradiction must be kept steadily in view in dealing with the ethical problem.

The attempt to combine together the Christian, the theological, ethic with general ethic is illustrated most signally in the Catholic doctrine of natural law. In this doctrine we are presented with two distinct ethical sciences combined together to make a unity. These two sciences are named moral philosophy and moral theology. They are distinguished from one another in method but united in essential content, inasmuch as the moral imperative, the "ought" is rooted in "being", in the nature of man and of things, while at the same time it is led through the light of revelation streaming in upon it.[1] Moral philosophy deals with the fundamental axioms of moral behaviour as taught by experience and history through the light of the natural reason. It regards these moral axioms as axioms of reason in the same sense as the axioms of logic are to be regarded as such. It knows them as the "ought" which is rooted in "being". But at the same time it recognizes that the reason would fall into error if it were not led by the light of revelation. Thus, the moral good as expressed by the four cardinal virtues, justice, temperance, prudence, fortitude, is rooted in man's nature and being, and can be discovered there by reason acting alone, and in independence of revelation. But the moral good, in this sense, is only the relatively good, and needs to be crowned and completed by the absolute good which is given in revelation. Moral philosophy, accordingly, must be supplemented by and integrated into moral theology, which alone is competent to deal with the absolute good. The theological virtues, faith, hope, and charity which are the fruits of supernatural grace cannot be established from the side of natural reason. Nevertheless they are the expressions of the natural reason when it is elevated into the sphere of grace. The distinctively Christian ethic thus forms the superstructure of an edifice of which general ethic is the sub-structure, and is unitary with it. The favourite watchword of this attempt to solve the ethical problem by linking on the distinctive Christian ethic to general ethic is "grace does not destroy but perfects nature".

[1] pp. 586 ff.

At first sight this is a very attractive solution and it has been worked out in Catholic theology with great precision and skill. It seems to offer a place where ethics as a human science, and ethics as resting on God's revealed will and commandment, can meet. It seems to put the Christian ethic in a position of authority and rule, while, at the same time, making room for and supplying justification of man's own independent ethical endeavour. It roots law in the nature of things, and yet exalts it over nature. The "ought" and the "is" are seen in each other and through each other.[1]

But, attractive as the theory is, it cannot be accepted. For this Catholic integration of moral theology with moral philosophy rests upon the fundamental view of a harmony established in "being", as such; between nature and super-nature, reason and revelation, man and God.[2] But this supposed harmony is surreptitiously brought in, and it can find no justification in the Biblical witness to revelation. Wherein lies the agreement between a presupposed harmony between man and God rooted in the fact that they both share in "being" and that harmony restored by God in His *deed* of reconciliation in Jesus Christ? Can a metaphysic of being make clear a harmony that has to be established by God's own action?[3] Furthermore, how can an "ought" which is fundamentally identical with "being" be a real "ought"? How can a law which is rooted in man's nature be a real command? If the "ought" is to be a genuine ought, it must come from without, it must be command; it must be the word of a Lord; it must be given to man, and it must not be compromised by being changed, however circumspectly, into an "is".[4] Or, rather, we shall say, the "is" from which it proceeds must be the "is" of God, and in no way the "is" of man; an "is" which is such in virtue of a great decision in which God's own being is determined, and which, therefore, determines the decisions, and so the being, of man. The pure idea of being or nature enfolding both God and man, "being" in abstraction from action and decision, can afford no ground from which to interpret either grace or command. Everything is here compromised. God and man are confounded together. Grace ceases to be grace, and command to be command.

[1] p. 587   [2] p. 588   [3] p. 589   [4] p. 591

A brief comment may be made here before we pass on. Trenchant as is Barth's criticism of the whole concept of natural law, he has no wish to conduct a direct campaign against it. As in the case of natural theology in general, he knows that it can be overthrown only by revelation itself. Unless it be perceived in the light of revelation to be man's attempt to justify himself and his world; unless it be seen to be the fruit of man's withdrawal into an independent position with regard to God's election of grace and the commandment which this brings with it—a position from which he strives, out of himself, to establish the ethical good—natural law will remain and perhaps ought to remain. Anyone, therefore, who seeks to combat Barth's criticism should not deal with it directly and independently, but in the whole context of the positive exposition which Barth presents. By the validity or otherwise of this, the question of natural law will be decided. Undoubtedly Barth's ethical teaching means a crisis in ethical thought, a crisis which will sooner or later have to be faced. Well-nigh everywhere, and in the Church perhaps specially, the presupposition holds that the moral basis of life is laid in the nature of things, and specifically in the nature of man, and that this nature is the object of direct investigation by the reason.[1] The actual empirical subject, man and his history, will, it is assumed, yield the data with which ethical doctrine can be constructed. That this subject is to be disqualified as fallen subject—that it is attacked by the commandment of God, that the true subject must be sought in a transcendence of the actual subject—is an idea to which, even in Christian circles, little more than lip-service is paid. It is widely supposed that all that is needed is to quicken and vivify the moral consciousness of the actual empirical subject. From this point of view, it is impossible to see how redemption can hold that radical significance which it possesses in Christianity. If, on the other hand, redemption does possess this radical significance, it is evident that the entire ethical question must be formulated in a new way, and that ethics, as it is generally pursued, must come to an end. Naturally, Barth does not think it possible,

[1] "In current belief there is a natural ethic and there is a Christian in parallelism; and between them conscience comes to the ground, distracted and unsure." Forsyth, The Justification of God, p. 106

or even desirable, to bring it to an end by means of direct attack. Even the theological ethic can only bear witness to the true answer to the ethical problem. It cannot of itself bring this answer on to the field. Only revelation itself can do that.[1] But what is to be expected of theological ethic is that it should bear this witness; in other words, that, like theology in general, it should be an act of pure obedience to the Word of God.

It is necessary to stress this, because, even in Christian circles, the general if unconfessed idea is that other considerations, besides that of obedience to the Word of God, must be kept in view in ethical thinking. The eye is continually on the prospects of ethics in general. Men ask how ethics can be justified before the world if it is not broad-based on nature. Will not an exclusive insistence on theological ethic lead to the conclusion that life outside the Christian sphere possesses no real standards and no real imperatives? Anxiety, nervousness, and not that faith that knows no anxiety save the all important and at last all inclusive one of obedience to the Word of God, holds back even Christian thinkers from taking the true line which alone holds promise for the world, and drives them to all kinds of compromises and weakenings. Just as in the realm of theology proper, anxiety for man's rights as a thinker distorts and perverts the witness to revelation and leads to a nervous apologetic which has neither savour nor salt, so, here, anxiety about the rights of man as ethical subject dims and darkens the true, the Christian ethic. If Christianity is to renew its life it must resolutely turn its back on this faithless anxiety. Only so will it shine out as the true light in a dark world.

But, to resume: we cannot hope to make headway in our discussion of the ethical problem unless we lay supreme emphasis on God as man's absolute Lord.[2] The being of God can in no way be abstracted from the life in which He exercises Lordship over the life of man. Incidentally, that excludes any conception of man's being as analogous to God's. But it includes the fact that man's being can in no wise be abstracted from the life in which he stands under God's Lordship. Man

---

[1] *Dog.*, II, 1, p. 571   [2] p. 594

"is" either obedient or disobedient in relation to God. Obedience or disobedience is his "being". No human action is independent or neutral. It follows therefore that the good cannot be a mere possibility. The good exists, and it is not a matter of our question or choice. And the good has been actualized; actualized in the event of Christ, in His life, death, and resurrection; actualized in the fact that Jesus Christ, as the subject of the divine election, is Himself man's justification and sanctification. All Christian exposition of ethic must be, above all, exposition of the word and work of God given in Jesus Christ. It cannot consist in the setting forth of any exemplary character amongst men which might be made the subject of investigation.[1] It cannot even be any ideal picture of Christian life which we might frame. Jesus Christ is Himself both the sanctifying God and the sanctified man; and man is sanctified, that is, he lives the true ethical life only through faith in Him. The law of God stands, we may say, because God is the doer of the law; because God commands only on the ground that He has Himself fulfilled what He has commanded. God's actualization and fulfilment of His own law, which is His work of grace for man, is the setting up of His claim over man.

When this is recognized, we are in a position to see both the content of the divine claim itself and the form in which it reaches us. The content may be described thus: human action is right action, that is, obedient action, in so far as it is an acknowledgment of and a testimony to the right of God's action.[2] No action which proceeds simply out of man's independent choice and volition, no action which is a mere conformity with principles which man sets up from his own centre, and as the result of his own free investigation of the nature of ethical action, can be the right action. The right action has already been accomplished in perfection and fullness by God, and man's action can only be right as it witnesses it and mirrors it. This it is permitted to do. Clearly there can be no thought of coercion here. Man is delivered from all coercion and constraint, is set free from every bondage of necessity which the world or his own nature would fasten upon him, and permitted an action which testifies to that divine action

[1] p. 597   [2] p. 638

which is above all necessity or constraint.[1] We describe, therefore, the form in which the divine claim reaches us as a permission. It guards and guarantees to man's life a genuine freedom.

We may illustrate the freedom which is the form in which the divine command comes to us very simply. Our life is set in the midst of many necessities and constraints which impose themselves on us as commands which have to be obeyed. There are, for example, the primitive necessities of eating, drinking, sleeping, and so on. On the higher levels, there are logical necessities, the necessities of thought which come to us in a commanding way: I must believe that twice two make four; that the two sides of a triangle are greater than the third side. Now, undoubtedly, the command of God comes to us in the sphere within which we have to live our life; comes to us, therefore, embedded, so to speak, within these necessities. But it comes to us in another form than these. It comes to us not as coercion but as permission. I *must* eat and drink; but my eating and drinking *may* become for me not merely a necessity but an ethical action. I may eat and drink, as Paul says, to the glory of God. My eating and drinking may become for me an act of thanksgiving. It may be an expression of the fact that, since God has chosen me for Himself, He bids me and permits me to live. It may be an acknowledgment that what God has done is right. The point is, that it is just in that region where mere necessity is transcended, where the bonds of mere coercion are broken, that the commandment of God operates, and its form as permission and freedom becomes manifest.

Again, my thinking must be determined by the law that twice times two make four, that the two sides of a triangle are greater than the third side, and so on. But my acknowledgment of this may become no mere bowing before an iron law. It may become an acknowledgment of the sovereignty of God, who, in the determinations which make up His own life and being, has granted a reflexion of these determinations within the created order, in order that man may be a rational being and so correspond with his mind with the wisdom of God. Thus, the commandments of God, while they come to man as he stands

[1] p. 651

94

within the whole complex of those laws, forces, and urgencies which make up his life in this world, being the commandments of God and not these laws, forces and urgencies in themselves, assure man's freedom; a freedom which becomes actual only in his faith. At the same time, they are verily *commandments*, and they bring all human action under responsibility.

And here a further observation calls to be made. Inasmuch as all our decisions and actions as men are rooted in a prior decision and action of God, inasmuch as they are responses either of obedience or disobedience to this decision and action, we cannot think of God's commandment as consisting in a mere code of moral rules, laws, and prescriptions, as such, and in abstraction from the presence and action of the person of the commanding God. In the strict sense, there are no commands of God which are such, merely in themselves; there is only the God who commands. In other words, the will of God is given in the actual concrete situations in our life which call for decision.[1] It is not as if there were the will of God on the one hand and the will of man on the other, and, in between, the commandment of God, which man acting purely from his own centre might obey or disobey. Man's self-determination in decision and action cannot act in independence of God's self-determination. Here and now, in the place and at the time in which I stand, I am called to hear and to obey the commandment of God. And my actual choice and action here and now are placed by God under His judgment and under His grace. Even the ten commandments and the sermon on the mount, understood as literal prescriptions, are not to be simply equated with the command of God. They point rather to the sphere, and indicate the direction, in which the commanding God moves and acts. The ten commandments are all bound up with God's choice of His people and His presence and action among them. They indicate, not a law-giver in the ordinary sense of the word, but a present rule and lordship. And the sermon on the mount stands in closest connection with the kingdom of God as event in the world.[2] They, therefore, mark out a sphere from which the commandment of God for me to-day can be heard. But His actual command is given me here and

[1] p. 738   [2] pp. 751 ff.

95

now in the crises which call upon me for concrete decision. In these crises I am not left without guidance. I belong to a people, I am a member of a Church which God's election of grace has called into being, and in the decisions and confessions of this Church I find indications of the nature of God's will. But not by following these, as such, and not even by conforming with the prescriptions of the ten commandments or the sermon on the mount, am I obeying the will and command of God. They will help me when I find myself set in the crisis of decision. But only in that crisis itself is the commandment of God given for me.

It follows, therefore, that we are not to think of the commandments of God as affording simply general principles, the actual working out of which might be left to man's own disposal and competence.[1] That would leave man at last master of the situation. It would dissociate the determinations of his life from the determinations of God and leave them under man's own control. He would be confronted with a programme over which he could exercise disposal. Within a wide circle of existence he would be his own lord and master. But since the whole man, man in his being and existence, is determined by God in His election of grace, there can be no action or decision of his life which is simply autonomous and independent. We must, therefore, think of the command of God as giving definite and concrete directions to every man in every decision of his life, and true ethical behaviour consists in a continuous activity of listening on the part of man to the word and commandment of God. This activity is best indicated by the word "responsibility".[2] And this responsibility will show itself in the fact that I, who have to decide and act to-day, and in view of the decisions which I shall be called upon to take to-morrow, allow the Word of God to call in question my acts and decisions of yesterday, that I refer them all to the judgment and the grace of God. I can never regard any of my acts and decisions, however right and justified they may seem to me to be, as simply identical with the will and command of God. The ethical question must be, for me, ever an open question, open not in the sense that the answer to it is still to seek as if it had not

[1] p. 739   [2] pp. 713 ff.

96

already been given, but open in the sense that it is always the question as to whether or how far my ethical action has been such as to give the right to the action of God. It is God who alone can justify our ethical action, and it is precisely that fact that places all our life under responsibility.

There is one misunderstanding which must here be guarded against. It might appear from the interpretation of God's command, as given to each man in the special, concrete, crises and decisions of his own life, as if we were, so to speak, atomizing God's commandment, destroying its unity, making it correspond to, and even identifying it with, a multitude of different life situations. The inference might be drawn that there was a special law for special people, special times, and special stages of culture. This inference would, however, be wholly incorrect. The divine commandment is the commandment of the one God, springing from the one election of grace, which includes all men and is directed to every situation. It therefore possesses at all times the same character and the same quality. It is always friendly to man, always beneficial to his life, always seeks his good.[1] It therefore promotes fellowship among men, and is a power making for the unity of mankind. The man who hears and obeys the divine commandment will ever move towards his fellow-man in friendship, and will always strive after his full well-being.[2] Where the moral law is made to consist in general rules and prescriptions whose particular and individual application is left over to man's disposal and choice, it inevitably divides men. The real decisions become the affairs of different men, classes, and stages of life. One man's right is set over that of another, and there is no way out of the situation save by conflict. But the command of God is always and everywhere the action of the one gracious God upon man's life, and this draws men together in unity and fellowship.

Moreover, the law of God, since it is always the action of the one God, unites a man within himself. The tragic disunity of life in general is due to the fact that man is not at one within himself. He brings to society a disunited self.[3] What wonder then that the relations of men with one another should mirror this disunited self! The individual personal man is a mass of

[1] p. 791   [2] p. 801   [3] pp. 812 f.

G

97

instincts, appetites, urges, desires, and needs, which war with one another. Now one of these is in the ascendant, and now another. To-day he will crave after intellectual satisfaction, and to-morrow after emotional. Now the needs of the body, now those of the mind, and now those of the soul, will sway him. And he lives his life in a discontinuous complexity of modes of being. He is citizen, he is family man, he is man of industry, of science, of art; he is sensual man, he is moral man, he is religious man. His life sways, oscillates, and is torn between values of the most divergent kind. Never does he reach the point where these aspects and modes of his life coalesce and unite. Only as the command of God descends upon him as action in all the decisions which make up his existence, is he brought to inner rest and harmony. Only so will he bring to society a sanctified self, a self which has in all its aspects renounced autonomy and independence, and so mirrors and radiates social unity and fellowship.

It will be seen, therefore, that the difference between individual and social ethics is transcended in the commandment of God. The various orders that arise in the evolution of man's social life and history, marriage, the state, industry, cultural developments, and the like, inasmuch as they are all bound up with a world which stands under God's election of grace, receive from that grace a relative justification and a relative sanctification. But this justification and sanctification can only be relative. These orders can be called ordinances of God only if it be understood that God is their Lord and not their hypostatization. They cannot be left to themselves and to the immanent laws and principles at work within them. Only in so far as they form a sphere in which the Word of God can be freely proclaimed and heard, a sphere which presents no hindrance but every opportunity to the Word of God's electing grace, do they become themselves truly justified and sanctified. Social ethics, together with individual ethics, arise from God's justification alone. It has no claim to independent consideration and can of itself establish no principles of binding obligation.

In his ethical life, man stands both nearer to and farther from God than in any other aspect of his existence. He stands nearer, in that his ethical life is a great searching and striving after justification. He stands farther, inasmuch as that same ethical life is shown in the light of the Cross of Christ to be vitiated by a great perversion; it is a continual fleeing from the justification of God. It becomes the great righteousness when it permits the judgment of God, which, in Christ's Cross becomes event as a radical judgment, to be passed upon it. Standing under that judgment it is wholly justified. The judgment of God does not happen in vain. It has a purpose and an end.[1] Man is justified by faith in Jesus Christ, in order now to be for ever bound to God and to live from Him. It is thus that his sanctification takes place. It is thus that God's action in choosing him for His own becomes the truth about his life. It is thus that he is placed under the promise of eternal life and moves forward and onward to a participation in the fullness of the blessedness of God.

POSTSCRIPT

IN our exposition of Barth's doctrine of God we have, of necessity, confined ourselves to the merest outlines. We have not been able to find room for his appraisement of the authorities, both ancient and modern, quoted by him; his critical analyses of contrasted views; and, more important still, the massive scriptural exegesis which he brings to the support of the positions upheld. The omission of this last, in particular, must mean a serious deficiency in the exposition. It is hoped, however, that Barth's volumes may be translated into English in the not too far-distant future. The slight sketch which we have given may serve the purpose of providing a kind of background from which the wide ramifications of the argument when it appears in its English dress may be surveyed.

We conclude with a brief comment. It is impossible to proceed far along the road of life without discovering that we may not believe what we like and we may not do as we please. We may believe only what is true, and we may do only what is right. But what ought we to believe and what ought we to do? What is truth and what is righteousness? The question, when we lift it into the light of God's revelation, narrows itself down

[1] pp. 854 ff.

99

to this: do we in all our thoughts and actions move within a sphere of pre-determining thoughts and actions, in which case they may become genuinely authorized, and validated as truth and right; or must we for ever see ourselves involved in a chaos of mere phenomena and the ideas which seek to interpret them—phenomena and ideas the relationships between which we are incapable of fixing with confidence and finality—in which case our quest for truth and right can at last be nothing but, at best, a highly-complicated game? Theology can only bear witness to the fact that the former of the two alternatives conveys the true answer. It cannot, however, be itself the true answer. Only revelation can be that. God declares that He Himself is the truth and the righteousness for man. Theology can but interpret that declaration in terms available to our understanding. It may be doubted whether it has ever done this with greater thoroughness and consistency than in the work of Karl Barth.

Part Two

THEOLOGICAL ESSAYS

I

REFORMATION ISSUES TO-DAY

By JOHN McCONNACHIE, D.D.

How was it that in the day of the Reformation the well-spring
of evangelical truth, so long silted up and covered over with
tradition and superstition, began again to flow so mysteriously
in all its ancient power, as if touched by some hidden wand?
What was the power which brought the Christian Faith back
to its essential principles—the Word of God and faith—that is,
back to itself?

Only what Calvin wrote in 1543 to Charles V, the antagonist
of the Reformation Movement, can explain it: "The Reformation of the Church is God's work, and is as much independent
of human life and thought as the resurrection of the dead, or
any such work is."

As a movement in history, the sixteenth-century Reformation
is now behind us. We shall not pass that way again. But as
a movement of the Spirit of God it has for us values which
remain. For Reformation according to the Word of God is
the law of the Church's life, and the Church's Theology.

No one has done more to reinterpret, transform, and illumine
the issues of the Reformation for our day than Karl Barth.

Important and determinative for all time, in virtue of its
hidden quality, as Barth recognizes the Reformation to be,
he clearly perceives that something more is required than
a mere re-publishing of the substance of Reformed Theology
to meet the twentieth century. It has to be re-examined,
scrutinized, in the light of the Word of God, and remoulded in
close relationship with the circumstances of our day.

That is the task which he is now pursuing as his life-work
—the presentation of an Evangelical and Church Dogmatics
which is, in the first place, a confession of his own meditation
on the faith of the Christian Church.

Some may regret that he has put off the prophet's mantle

and transformed the message of his *Romans* into a dogmatic and ethical system: but he himself feels the obligation as a theologian to express the Word of God, as it has come to him, in terms of human thought.

His use of such philosophical words as *Hohlraum* and *Todeslinea* did their service in an earlier day, he says, but "it would be tedious and confusing to use them now". Also what was earlier described as "the theology of crisis" is "now behind", he says. "It could not and ought not to last longer than a moment." He has also abandoned the use of the phrase "Wholly Other" because his critics misunderstood it. The teaching in his Church Dogmatics is become, therefore, less distinctive but more mature.

So much has been written of "Barthianism", as if it were some strange, foreign heresy, that it would be well for us to remind ourselves, in the first place, how much of the substance of Reformed Theology Barth has taken up into his Dogmatics. With all the fundamental doctrines of the Reformers he is in general agreement. While his own origins are in Calvin, he has drawn liberally on Luther, combining what is best in both Reformers. Luther's doctrine of the free Grace of God in Jesus Christ, a God who "reveals Himself in hiddenness and hides Himself in His Revelation", he sets forth in glowing terms. He speaks now more freely of the *Love of God*, devoting a whole long section to "the Being of God as the Loving One" (*Dog.* II, 1, 36). To Luther also he goes for his doctrine of Scripture, avoiding Calvin's leaning to the infallibility of the written word. To him, as to Luther, "The Scripture is the cradle wherein the Christ is laid."

He is at one with the Reformers, especially Luther, and against the Schoolmen, in holding that the Bible is not a depository of propositions, but that in it we have the personal revelation of a God who has spoken, speaks, and will speak to men, as he spoke in early days to the prophets and apostles. With the Reformers, he draws a distinction between the Word of God and Scripture, affirming the great Reformed doctrine of the *testimonium Spiritus Sancti internum* through which the Scripture becomes always event—a *dandum*, not a *datum*.

We owe it to Barth, indeed, that he has done much to

restore in our time the distinction between the true Reformed doctrine of the Word and that Calvinistic orthodoxy of a later day, which, falling back into Catholicism, conceptualized the Bible into beliefs and propositions and lost the early insight of the first Reformers of the dialectical character of Biblical truth.

In common with the Reformers, and against the Schoolmen, particularly Aquinas (whom he reckons next to Calvin as the greatest of theologians), he holds that we have no real knowledge of God outside His Word. The *imago Dei* has been so corrupted by sin, infecting the whole nature of man, reason, will, and heart, that any natural continuity of man with God is put out of court. Jesus Christ is the one sure Word of God.

The old controversy as to whether there is a general as well as a special revelation, which has occupied the mind of the Church since the days of Augustine, came under review at the Reformation and was left an open question. Calvin believed that "there is a sense of Deity naturally engraven on the human heart", and allowed a place for "a small flame" (*scintilla*) of natural knowledge of God, but "not such as to enable it to comprehend God". Here, Barth, as we shall see, has sharpened the issue by his refusal to allow a place for any Natural Theology *in the Church*.

Along with the Reformers, Barth accepts the Nicene doctrine of the Person of Christ, approaching it, however, as they did, through His atoning work, and not from any previously thought-out idea of what Godhead and manhood must be, and how they became united in the Incarnation. His approach, as that of the Reformers, is dynamic and functional; not static and metaphysical.

He gives the same central place to the experience of justification by faith alone, which, as we shall see, he makes the basis of his whole teaching on Christian ethics. And he uses the word "experience" more freely than he formerly did, believing that there is now less likelihood of it being misunderstood.

In common with the Reformers, Barth holds the doctrine of the Church as a *communio sanctorum*, the new Israel of God, a holy people depending on the purpose of His will, independent of all visible organizations, and yet also a Visible Society to be seen wherever the Word of God is faithfully preached, the sacraments celebrated, and the fruits of the Spirit manifested in the world.

Only in one doctrine, apart from Natural Theology, to which we shall refer later, does Barth make any serious departure from the teaching of the Reformers. It is in relation to the doctrine of Election. He finds in Calvin a determinism by which God appears to make Himself the prisoner of His own pre-destination. To Barth, Election, which he links closely with Christology, is not a determinism, a mystery lying behind the Gospel and threatening its nature as gospel, it is rather the sum of the Gospel. It is a decision of God's grace to choose man, everyman, unless a man finally refuses, and even in hell he will not be beyond the grace of God. Even the reprobation of a man would be grounded on God's grace, since He has not two wills, as Barth emphasizes, but one will.

By exposing Calvin's error of making a distinction between God's decree, and the holy mystery of Jesus Christ, and of seeking the explanation of Predestination in a Divine determinism which took place in some eternity before and without Christ, Barth has rendered a real service to the Church. He has clarified this Reformation issue, and provided a conception of Election in which the Christian mind can permanently rest. It is from this meeting-place of God's decision, and man's election in Jesus Christ, that Barth, as a theologian, makes his start in his great attempt to provide for the Church a Christian Dogmatic for to-day.

The "Barthian" theology, so-called, is thus seen to be a summons *ad fontes*—back to the springs of the Reformed doctrine of Revelation as the Word of God; back to the Reformed doctrine of the Church as the Church of the Word; back to the New Testament and Reformed doctrine of justification by faith alone; as providing the only right ethic and true motive to the obedience of a Christian man. But it is also, in the second place, a summons to a re-thinking, re-casting, and correcting of those doctrines in the light of the New Testament and in the light of to-day. The Reformed issues are, therefore, threefold: theological, ecclesiastical, and ethical.

(1) *Theological Issues*

Barth's fundamental concern is with the true meaning of Revelation which he regards as critical, vitally affecting, as it does, not only Christian but profane thought, and raising problems of the most decisive character. Does the Christian Church, which claims to have a unique Gospel, and a Universal Mission, rest on a Divine Absolute, a Word of God, or is it merely a human institution called forth in answer to human desires and needs.

Modern liberal theology, in Barth's view, yielded too easily to the spirit of the Age which led it to take a very exaggerated estimate of the potentialities of human nature. The Jesus of History was preached as a Teacher and Reformer rather than as a Saviour. The urgency of Christianity, as a Gospel of Redemption, was obscured. The very idea of Revelation as the Word of God had faded out of the minds of many, and the term itself was used in so vague a sense, and applied to so many things, such as science, art, human love, that it had ceased to have any well-defined meaning. Any human experience, which went deep enough, was dignified by the name "revelation".

This theology sought its point of departure in a religious *a priori* within the soul of man, a God-consciousness which belonged to man as man. It postulated a deep and abiding continuity between the Divine and the human spirit. Everyman, at the centre of his personality, was in contact with God and therefore could pass from experience (the known) to God (the unknown) and, in his religious experience, find peace. It made much also of the *revelatio naturalis*, claiming that the best available clue to the being and nature of God was to be found in the higher elements of human experience, in the will, reason, and conscience, even in the milk of human kindness, because of this kinship (*analogia entis*) between God and man.

Arguing thus, from man to God, from human values to the Divine, it believed that it could apprehend the Supreme Being. Religion became thus, like science, a way to the knowledge of God. Human discovery and Divine revelation were complementary sides of the self-same fact of experience. There might be a difference of degree but there was no difference of kind between revelation and other human knowledge. All truths were both discovered and revealed. Revelation was everywhere, if only we had eyes to see it. History was the gradual progressive revelation of God in the human spirit. Divine revelation completed itself, not in a break with the natural and spiritual conceptions of man, but in a continuation of them. It consisted in extending, deepening, and clarifying the religious consciousness.

In this prevailing immanentist and humanistic theology, backed up as it was by its alliance with a philosophical idealism which had been accepted as an ally against naturalism, but which turned out to be a traitor, Barth recognized a serious challenge to the Reformed doctrine of Revelation as the Word of God. It had surrendered its unique quality and lacked the independence and authority which a true theology of the Word should possess. Barth saw in it a falling back to the teaching of Thomas Aquinas, and the Schoolmen. It was the old, yet ever present, tendency to hellenize the Christian faith; the tendency to seek a complete view of reality and to bring the Christian view into line with it. It was the attempt, such as Aquinas made in his day, to provide a synthesis between man's natural knowledge of God, and his knowledge won by Revelation.

He thus found himself committed to a battle on two fronts —first, against liberal Protestant theology, and secondly, against Medieval theology, between which he discovered many striking resemblances. That of neo-Protestantism he counted the greater defection, due to its complete surrender to the *analogia entis*. Aquinas and the Schoolmen did believe that there was a difference between the approach to God by man, and the approach by God to man. Whether the Divine initiative relativized the achievements of man's moral effort, as in Calvinism, or whether it confirmed and completed them, as in Thomism, it did, in its transcendent givenness, cut athwart them. But neo-Protestantism, in its readiness to capitulate to modern thought, had identified the approach by man to God, and the approach by God to man, as if they were but two aspects of the one experience.

From these attempts, both medieval and modern, to reach God through the mind of man, despite the bridges that are never really spanned, Barth has called for a return to the Reformed doctrine of Revelation as the Word of God, which he believes to be that of the New Testament witness. The Christian Revelation, he maintains, makes a positive break with all religious *a priori*. The first fundamental fact of which faith knows is that there is no immanent continuity between man and God. There is a discontinuity, due to sin, which has broken the original life-unity of the Creator and the creature. It is moral, not ontological, brought about by man's refusal of God, who has thus become, as Barth puts it: "Other to us, when He is yet related to us." "The boulder of a *Thou* which does not become an *I* is cast in our path." Man's true response to God, then, is not some religious instinct, but a response called forth by the Creative Spirit Himself, whose first gift is the faith to receive it.

Something should be said at this point of this conception of Revelation as "the Word of God", and whence it comes. Its origin is, of course, in the Scriptures. It was through a creative Word of God, a Word which was also an Act, that the worlds were made. It was through the same creative Word that man came into existence. It was a creative Word of God given to them, which they knew to be not their own, that the prophets spoke. And the final unfolding of that Word was when "the Word became flesh and dwelt among us." God's original relation to the world, therefore, is a personal relation which can best be expressed by this term, *Word*. It is the means by which He reveals His personal nature. It is always the word of a *Thou* to an *I*—the two spiritual realities of life. The *I* can only be understood in relation to the *Thou*. In its last ground our spiritual relation to God is that of the true *Thou* to the true *I*.

The term "Word of God", therefore, best conveys all that the New Testament means by revelation. It is not a mere opening of the eyes, but a giving of God. It is not a human, but a Divine, event; not a continuity, but a discontinuity with what is human; not a mere subjective experience, but a truth which is experienced. It is not something natural, but supernatural. It is not man seeking reality, but Reality seeking man. It is a real *coming* of God into the world, an encounter with God who is Other than the world, while yet related to it as Creator, a Divine Action upon the world. When the Word became flesh it laid hold on our humanity, even on our flesh of sin, and spoke the redeeming Word, a Word from beyond to which we have no access, since only God can speak of God, a Word which ever remains dynamic, and is never static.

The New Testament refuses to make anything in the world, or in man, the *seat* of revelation, not even the conscience, until it is illumined by the Holy Spirit. There is no such thing as revelation *per se*. There is no revelation of God which *resides*, as such, in man, either in his mind, or heart, or human values, although the Holy Spirit can make all of these to be organs through which He declares His mind. There is no revelation of God which resides, as such, even in the historical Jesus. That which the historian sees is not the saving revelation of God. The true knowledge of God, mediated to us through Jesus Christ, His Son, comes by way of crisis, event, and decision of faith. Revelation is a personal, dynamic Word, the first act of which is to work the miracle of faith for its reception. It is never a religious idea, a *semper et ubique*, but a contingent, contemporaneous word, and faith is that which binds man, the *I*, to the Divine *Thou*. It is a self-evidencing word which shines by its own light. It is always a hidden word which reaches us in a broken indirect way. Even in Jesus Christ, the Word of God appeared *incognito* in the worldly form of a servant.

Finally, revelation is a last word, not in the sense of being the last word in a historical sequence, but in an eschatological sense, as the breaking in of the new world of God, the world of the resurrection, into time. It is the event which brings all history, as well as every religion, including the Christian religion, into judgment. However many beautiful thoughts the great ethnic religions contain, as they do, however exalted be the characters they have produced, they must all come to the crisis of the Cross and Resurrection, and be viewed and judged in the light of Him who is the light of the World.

We cannot then parley with the Word of God. It is not something we possess, but something which possesses us. It can never belong to the sphere of human having, but implies a life of repeated decisions in order to retain it. It is true that we *grow* in grace and in the knowledge of our Lord and Saviour

Jesus Christ. But the line of our growth to that goal, like every other line, consists of points, events, decisions, in that dialectic of permanency and event which constitutes the Christian life.

To the criticism, often made, that this "Barthian" doctrine of revelation is atomistic, that it views the "good life", so-called, not as character or purpose but as "a series of jerks", Barth has two things to say. First, the "good life" is not our life, the life of the *Ego*, but the life which God lives in us, and for us, through His Holy Spirit—a life in which we are not left without guidance and direction. The permanent content of faith is the *abiding* Christ. "I am the Vine, ye are the branches." Further, Barth replies that while it is true that man lives, in great and in small things, in ever new decisions, "we do not", he says, "live as atoms each for himself. We live in the Church, in a definite Christian tradition. We have passed through a definite Christian education, we have a Catechism, we have a dogma, we have definite knowledge passed on by the Church. We have fathers in the faith."

Another criticism, equally groundless, frequently made against the "Barthian" conception of revelation is that it is irrational. In the Christian Revelation we are certainly dealing with a knowledge of God which is in no wise founded in man, and which by no means is to be obtained by man through his rational faculties. It is a knowledge of God which, says St. Paul, "transcends all our powers of thought" (Philippians, 4: 7). But for it to be *beyond* the natural reason does not make it in any way *against* reason. Reason has its limits. As the highest faculty of man it is indispensable, and, within its own sphere, it is autonomous. Its sphere is the world of empirical knowledge, of life and consciousness. But man, through sin, has fallen out of the world of the Divine Intention in which he was created, and the light of the creative *logos* has been darkened. It can be assumed that there are many things which he can think correctly, but he is incapable by any rational capacity of his own to come to God. *God must first speak.* Man needs revelation to deliver him from the unconditioned need of his existence. His reason, as having part in the brokenness of human existence, itself needs renewal, that "renewing of the mind or reason" by the Holy Spirit, of which St. Paul speaks (Romans 12: 2). Then only can it take up into itself, and understand, and explain the Divine Revelation in terms of human thought.

But any final divorce, or opposition, between reason and revelation is unthinkable. That would bring an unbearable cleft into human life. The Word of God, as Barth says, is a rational not an irrational event. It is the form in which Reason communicates itself to reason, Person to person. The human reason has, therefore, a task inside the sphere of Revelation which it receives at the hands of Revelation itself. Otherwise there could be no such thing as Dogmatics, in the sense in which Barth explains it as "the scientific test to which the Christian Church puts herself, as to the content of her singular speech about God" (*Dog.* I, 1, 2).

Barth himself makes the fullest use of his own acute reasoning powers. Yet he recognizes that, for him, as a theologian, reason has its bounds. Theology is the freest, but also the most bound, among the sciences. Its presupposition is the great redemptive Act of God in Jesus Christ. It cannot itself choose the truth to which it has to give value to the Church. It cannot regard itself as a general search for truth. It bows before the truth of Revelation. It listens-in to a conversation in which God speaks and man hears, and it gives its instruction in terms which can be understood. It has an authoritarian character, but only for faith. But that God has revealed Himself through His *Word*, a Word that can be expressed in terms of human thought, must indicate that He appeals to the reason which He has created, in so far as it can comprehend it.

Revelation and Natural Theology

It is a relevant question to ask: in what relation then does revelation, so understood, stand to Natural Religion, and Natural Theology? This much discussed question has been treated by Barth at length, and in a highly original way (*Dog.* II, 1, 132 f.).

While it occupied the minds of the Reformers they failed to think the whole relation out. They regarded the Natural Theology of Aquinas and the Schoolmen as resting on a radical error—the *analogia entis.* But they allowed a place to man's natural knowledge of God, without relating it to the central doctrine of their faith—justification by faith alone.

With more consistency, Barth starts off from the point of view of grace, of justification by faith alone, and carries it to its proper conclusion. He does not deny the existence of natural theology; indeed, he emphasizes its vitality in all ages. How could it have been otherwise? God has set the stamp of His creatorhood upon the world. There is a basic ontic continuity between man and God not destroyed by sin. Man's creatureliness remains, else there were no sin. Had God left no trace of Himself within the human consciousness, He would have been unknowable. "But in the readiness of God to be known", says Barth, "the readiness of man is also included."

Barth has avoided, although not all Barthians, the error of the medieval Nominalists of making man a creature cut off from God without any direct contact with Him possible. He admits that there is a voice in the cosmos the "echo" of which man can hear. But this origin in God is hidden and lost through man's sin, by which he has fallen out of continuity with God, so that it has become the problem of his life, and not its solution. Man's one remaining point of contact with God, which distinguishes him from the animal, is the distress of his existence, his divided life, his questing and questioning, his consciousness of perplexity, and darkness of mind, which he can in no wise answer or understand. "We ought", says Barth, "to be merciful and understand the fact—the fact itself is merciless enough —that the natural theology of the natural man is his only comfort in life and death, an insidious and perishable comfort, but that, man, as such, cannot perceive."

The real question, he says, is whether this natural theology is to be allowed a legitimate place *in the sphere of the Church.* His own view is that the proclamation of the Christian Church, and the theology of the Word of God which rightly understands itself, can have nothing to do with it, and has for it no use. The proclamation of the Church and its theology are occupied with the Word of God, and with Jesus Christ. It cannot serve two masters.

But why has the Church no use for it? Because, says Barth, something took place at the Incarnation and the Cross which has set the whole question on a new footing. With the coming of the revelation of Christ, we recognize that the voice in the cosmos is the voice of Christ, and, because the Christian hears that, he has no use for natural theology. It has been undermined and made impossible by the revelation of Christ. It is seen to be error when brought under the judgment of the Cross.

This is Barth's special contribution to the issue of natural theology. The passage often quoted as a Biblical foundation for natural theology (Romans 1: 17 f.) he shows to be an actual indictment of it. It is the "shadow-side" of the revelation of the Cross without the knowledge of which the "light-side" could not be understood (*Dog.* II, 1, 132). Barth's position, then, is not a factual, or metaphysical, denial of natural theology, but a repudiation of it, in so far as the Christian Church is concerned.

This was the ground for the strong resistance which Barth maintained against the "German Christians", so-called—the compromisers with Naziism—in their advocacy of natural theology, including race, soil, blood, and which took shape in the Barmen Confession of May 31, 1934, with its opening proclamation.

"Jesus Christ, as He is witnessed in the Scriptures, is the one Word of God which we have to hear and which in life and death we are bound to trust and obey. We condemn the false doctrine that the Church, as source of its message, can and must, beside this one Word of God, acknowledge as God's revelation such other facts and powers, forms and truths." Behind these words lay a bitter battle.

In concluding this section, we may say that the main theological issue to-day lies between those who hold by Calvin, called neo-Calvinists, and those who hold by Aquinas, called neo-Thomists. Is God the Lord, as Calvin maintains, transcendent, holy, separated from the world's sin by a gulf so great that it can only be bridged by Divine Grace? Or is there a continuity, and likeness, an *analogia entis*, between Creator and creature, even in his fallen condition, as Aquinas maintains. Thomism, and with it the whole Roman Catholic Church, holds that a natural knowledge of God by man is made possible even in his fallen state. Man is a rational animal, his nature is good, though not wholly good. But it has been spared a radical crisis. The bridge between God and man may be frail, but it remains unbroken. The supernatural can be reared upon the natural. As Aquinas puts it: *"gratia non tollit sed perficit naturam."*

Barth leaves us in no doubt as to where he stands. "I hold", he says, "the *analogia entis* to be the discovery of Anti-Christ." At the same time he acknowledges that there is an underlying forgotten truth of the creation suggested by the phrase: *analogia entis.* "In the *theologia revelata* is the *theologia naturalis*; in the reality of the Divine Grace is the truth of the Divine Creation comprehended. In this sense it is true that *gratia non tollit sed perficit naturam."*

(2) *Ecclesiastical Issues*

We turn now to the ecclesiastical issues of the Reformation, as Barth has illumined them. If he is a great Reformed theologian, he is also a great Reformed Churchman who never separates, even in thought, theology and Church. He knows that the Church did not begin at the Reformation, as some Protestants appear to imagine. He believes in the one, holy, Catholic Church, and serves himself heir to its great past, the ancient Catholic Church, the Church of the Fathers and the Creeds, the Medieval Church, as well as the Church of the Reformation. He reaffirms the purpose of the Reformers for a return to the New Testament conception of the Church, the Church of the Word, a Church of Sinners who have been justified by faith, a Church of the Mercy of God which seeks no power or glory of its own, and his call has been heard in every Protestant land.

He is himself a sturdy Protestant, but in the original meaning of the word. His protest is not against, but *for*, the Church, the true Church; which means that he is at the same time a good Catholic. True Protestantism does not signify that it is less, but more, not weaker but stronger: *Church*—the only Church he knows is a Church which is always engaged in a struggle for her true nature as the Church, which is always undergoing a

reformation according to the Word of God, and ever again
becoming Church, by bringing its members under the judgment
of the Word of God. The Church is, and remains true, only in so
far as Christ lives in it, and makes it subject to Himself. That
is the mystery of the Church. "When we enquire about the
Church," he says, "it is Jesus Christ who is the subject of our
enquiry."

Here, once more, Barth has had to fight a battle on two
fronts: first, against the neo-Protestant Church; and, second,
against the Roman Catholic Church.

He has little patience with modern Protestantism, maintaining that it has not only lost its authority as a Church, but
has given up the very substance of a Church. By going over to
the genial Protestantism of a Schleiermacher, it has passed
beyond recognition as a Church of the Word. Is it worth while
for it, he asks, to retain a separate existence? "If I came to
the conclusion", he writes, "that the interpretation of the
Reformation on the lines of Schleiermacher was right, I would
not become a Roman Catholic, but I would take farewell of
the Protestant Church, and being placed before the choice of
two evils I would choose rather to be a Roman Catholic."

His battle against Roman Catholicism he has conducted
with greater seriousness, and more respect for it as a Church,
with the result that he is one of the few Protestant theologians
whose work is carefully studied by Roman Catholic theologians.
With a great weight of knowledge, and remarkable freedom
from bias, he has sought to understand and judge the Roman
Catholic position, recognizing that he is dealing with a concern
of the faith common to both Protestants and Roman Catholics.
He has shown himself ready to learn from Anselm, Aquinas,
Bonaventura, etc., and distinguished Roman Catholic theologians, like Dr. Karl Adam, have honoured his work. Already in
1926 Dr. Adam wrote: "If orthodox Protestantism is to experience an awakening it will be by this theology."

He has assailed Roman Catholicism on two grounds. First,
that it is not truly Catholic; and, second, that it is not fully
Christian. He perceives in Roman Catholicism a strong in-
veterate enemy of evangelical religion which lacks the mark of
a true Catholicity in its refusal, by its very constitution, to

submit itself to self-examination in the light of God's Word. "God is not Lord in His own House." In her pride and self-assurance, Rome refuses to listen to Jesus Christ and let herself be judged by Him. While she lays claim to authority in virtue of the fact that Jesus is primarily the Acting One in the Church, she allows other authorities, such as natural law, and natural theology, to be set up alongside Jesus Christ.

His second ground of criticism is that the Roman Catholic Church is not fully Christian. He bases his argument on her subordination of the *analogia fidei* to the *analogia entis*, instead of subordinating the *analogia entis* to the *analogia fidei*. She gives thereby a naturalistic foundation to the Church, and not a spiritual; basing it, not only on Peter the man, but on Nature itself as something that is akin to the Divine.

The strong divergence between neo-Calvinists and neo-Thomists, to which we have referred as one of the main theological issues of the Reformation, is thus seen to be one of the main ecclesiastical issues of the Reformation which Barth has brought out clearly.

His main interest is not in divergence, but in unity; the unity of "the Church in the Churches". He has little faith in man-made unions of the Churches as a path to unity. It must come the other way round. Only in obedience to Jesus Christ, the Head, can unity of the Church be found. His voice and call, the voice of the Good Shepherd, alone can effect it.

(3) *Ethical Issues*

So complicated is the structure of modern society, so full of tensions and ethical antinomies, and what has been described as "frontier-situations", to say nothing about the present disintegration of life, even of the individual life, that any question of an absolute ethic may well seem vain. Is there, indeed, such a thing as a Christian ethic?

To the Reformers, there appeared to be little difficulty. They did not think of ethics as a problem to be solved but as a thank-offering of a life of faith and obedience for the forgiveness of God through Jesus Christ. By placing in the centre of their faith the doctrine of justification by faith alone, they brought the question of ethics—of what we ought to do—into the foreground as a question affecting each individual soul. Man's relation to God was now seen to be personal, and not legal. His standing before God was determined, not by any moral achievements of his own, but by the grace of God. Morality was secured by being transcended. It ceased to be a conscious effort and became the spontaneous expression of a sense of indebtedness to God.

But, just as in natural theology, so in ethics, the Reformers did not carry their doctrine to its final conclusion. They repudiated the medieval view that man can be sufficiently instructed in the right ethic by some *lex naturae*, supplemented by the revealed will of God. What heathen philosophy and medieval theology had sought in the idea of natural law, God had given in the *lex scripta*, in order, as Calvin said, "to remove the obscurity of the law of nature". Calvin was prepared, however, to grant that the Biblical ethic was, as he said, "grounded on the strange knowledge of God in nature".

This came of his determinist doctrine of predestination, which was based, not on Jesus Christ as the completion in time of God's original purpose and decision to save men, all men, but on a secret decree of God before the worlds began. He was thus led to go behind Christ and seek his basis for ethics, as for theology, in an absolute decree of God, the hidden God, which could only be known, so far as it could be known, in its reflection in natural law.

Barth has both sharpened and centralized this ethical issue of the Reformation. He refuses to seek any basis for ethics in natural law. "There is," he says, "no *lex naturae*. God is the *lex naturae*." He rejects any absolute decree which is not identical with the concrete decree of God in Jesus Christ for man's election. This enables him to shift the whole ground of ethics directly on to the action of God in Jesus Christ. Thus, the true Christian ethic, as man's response to the Word of Predestination, becomes event in Christ, and is seen to be a living Reformation issue to-day.

It is not for nothing that Barth, in his Dogmatics, follows up his doctrine of Election immediately by the Divine Commandment, bringing both together in his doctrine of God.

God cannot be thought of apart from that relation in which He has bound Himself to man, and man to Himself, in Christ. Election is the ground and presupposition of ethics. In choosing man in Christ Jesus, God lays His claim upon him. This is the ethical imperative, the one true Christian ethic for man. The content of the Gospel is this election in grace. The form of it is the Divine Commandment. God's election of grace is for all men in Christ. All men stand, whether they know it or not, whether they will it or not, within the scope of the Divine Election, and therefore under the Commandment of God, and responsible to His Law.

Barth examines the various systems of ethics, giving special and respectful study to the Roman Catholic doctrine of Natural Law, and he arrives at the conclusion that all systems fail in their ability to provide an authority, which is to be found neither outwardly in the world, nor inwardly in the heart, or will, or conscience. With the best will in the world man cannot arrive at the *ought*; not even Kant by his autonomous will and categorical imperative. So he goes back to the Pauline-Reformed doctrine of justification by faith in which he sees— granted a better formulation of it, and fuller unfolding of it than the Reformers achieved—the one possibility for contemporary man in his present confusion. The problem of ethics is the problem of the "sickness unto death" of man, who knows that he cannot save himself. Left to himself he is in no position to solve this problem of his existence. The offer of forgiveness is the one and only answer to the ethical question, which means that it can be answered only by the God of Grace.

With that perspective depth into the meaning of Christian doctrine which he possesses, Barth has gone down to the roots of the ethical problem, as the Reformers failed to do. Ethics is a personal problem to which there is but one answer. It is the problem of existence, of the reality of God, and of His judgment. It is not a question among other questions, but the question of human existence. How we will and what we do, *that we are*. It is not that a man exists, and then acts. He exists in that he acts. His activity is the forthgoing of his existence. The only true and absolute ethic for man, therefore, must be a theological ethic, grounded on justification by faith, that decisive experience in which the sovereign and loving God meets man in grace, and he responds in faith and obedience. By opening this way God has solved for man his insoluble problem—the problem of the ought, which is also the problem of the good.

Barth works out in detail this Christian ethics, which he calls "The Reality of the Divine Commandment", under three heads: The Commandment of the Creator; The Commandment of the Reconciler; the Commandment of the Redeemer. He believes that the Divine Commandment, when listened to, will yield not only general principles of life, but definite directions for life, in work, home, family, State and Church. Here, as in his theology, his activism comes into evidence. Ethics is no academic pursuit, no purely theoretic treatment of the ideal life. It has to do with society, even with political life and action. It makes its voice to be heard in the street. He is intensely aware of the ethical issues of to-day, in State and Church, having himself faced them, and suffered for them.

Our Ethic, he says, and this is his main emphasis, can come forth only as a thank-offering for the reconciliation achieved for us through Jesus Christ. "To believe in Jesus Christ means to be thankful." This must bring about, not merely a change of conduct and action, but a change of the being of man before God. The change from the impossible and dangerous stand of unthankfulness into thankfulness as something new and better, is the one possible and hopeful stand before God. There is nothing left to do for the creature who knows God but to thank and serve Him in a life of faith and obedience, "looking for and hasting unto the coming of the day of God". His last word is the eschatological Hope. "In hope we are the children of God."

II

THE WORD OF GOD AND THE NATURE OF MAN

Qui Deum vere colit atque honorat, in hominen contumeliosus esse verebitur.

CALVIN, in *Epist. Iacobi*, 3, 11.

By REV. T. F. TORRANCE, M.B.E., B.D.

AT no point is theology more relevant to-day than in the issues it raises about our knowledge of man. This essay is an attempt to set forth some of these issues, particularly as raised by John Calvin and brought to bear upon the thought of our own day by Karl Barth, against what they both believe to be an un-Biblical view of man.

Calvin laid it down from the very start that there can be no true knowledge of man except within our knowledge of God. For this reason, Reformed theology has always been shy about erecting an anthropology, not because it lacked a view of man, but because such a view cannot be enunciated as an independent article of faith as if it could of itself condition or contribute to our knowledge of God. On the other hand, it has always insisted that, unless our knowledge of God strikes home to us in such a way that we come to a true knowledge of ourselves, our knowing of God is not real. "Therefore it is evident that man never attains to a true self-knowledge until he has previously contemplated the Face of God, and come down after such contemplation to look into himself."[1] These words "come down" are important, for they indicate the essential direction and motion of all Christian thought. *In lumine tuo videmus lumen.*[2] They are also important, however, because it is upon this downward motion of God's grace that the very being of man is grounded. Therefore, while a Christian doctrine of man, like every other article of faith, is grounded upon the acknowledgment of a Revelation, in this instance the knowledge involved is essentially reflexive, both of a Word of God about Himself, and of the

---

[1] *Inst.*, I, 1, 2   [2] Psalm 36 : 9; cf. Calvin, *ad loc.*

creative activity of His love. Thus, what Calvin would have us
note at the outset of a doctrine of man is that the direction and
motion of our knowing must correspond with the essential
direction and motion of grace, for that is the ground of man's
existence as a being made to know God. Therefore we must try
to formulate a doctrine of man not by an activity which
inverts the motion of grace but by an activity which responds
to it. Inasmuch as "man is only an image in regard to God",[1]
though to image the glory and grace of God belongs to his
true nature as an intelligent being, we may know man truly only
in his existential answer to the Word of grace.

Calvin was fond of basing a discussion of the nature of man
on the statement of St. Paul that as men "we live and move and
have our being" in God.[2] Those words, he said, expressed the
three gradations of human existence. We have being in God in
the same sense as all other created being; and we have motion
or animation in the same sense as other living creatures; but
we have a higher life in God proper to us as men, in which life
is peculiarly matched to grace.[3] At this point Calvin laid great
stress upon the words of St. John's Gospel: "In Him was life,
and the life was the light of men."[4] Therefore, in describing
the Biblical account of creation, Calvin pointed out that man
was created in such a way as to be given a special relation to
the Word of God upon the communication of which he lives.
All things were indeed created by the Word, and maintained
in being by the Word, but man's true life consists in an
intelligent motion in answer to the action and Word of God's
grace. That is man's peculiar dignity, that, being under deeper
obligation, he might use his special endowments in thankful
acknowledgment of God's gracious Self-communication, and
that he might devote himself entirely to knowing God, and
meditating upon His perfections.[5] In that responsive motion
alone does man find his true life and destiny. Calvin has given a
particularly clear account of his views here when speaking about

[1] Pierre Maury, in *The Christian Understanding of Man* (Oxford Conference
series, No. 11, *The Church, Community, and State*), p. 252.
[2] Acts 17 : 28; and Calvin's *Comm.*, *ad loc.*
[3] Calvin, *Serm. on Job*, 10 : 7 f.
[4] John 1 : 4. See Calvin, *ad loc.* and *Serm. on Job*, 35 : 8 f.
[5] *Inst.*, I, 5, 9; I, 14, 21; *Comm. on Acts*, 17 : 27

the tree of life which was planted in the Garden of Eden. It was the intention of God that "as often as man tasted of the fruit of that tree, he should remember whence he received his life, in order that he might acknowledge that he lives not by his own power, but by the kindness of God alone; and that life is not (as they commonly say) an intrinsic good, but proceeds from God. . . . The life of all things was included in the Word, but especially the life of men, which is conjoined with reason and intelligence. . . . Wherefore by this sign, Adam was admonished that he could claim nothing for himself as if it were his own, in order that he might depend wholly on the Son of God, and might not seek life anywhere but in Him . . . He possessed life only as deposited in the Word of God, and could not otherwise retain it, than by acknowledging that it was received from Him."[1]

This means that, unlike the other creatures of the world, man lives truly as man only in conscious and thankful relation to the grace of God, and in the consciousness of his own creaturehood. It is here that we see the important part played by self-knowledge in Reformed theology, for it is only when a man knows himself to be a creature utterly dependent on the grace of God that he is able in his knowledge of God so to live in a thankful fashion corresponding with the motion of grace that he reflects in the mirror of his intelligent life the glory of God. That is man's chief end and true felicity. We may state this in other words by saying that man has been created an intelligent being in order to know God in such a way that in the act of knowing man is brought to re-live consciously, and in a qualitatively different fashion, the very movement of grace in which he is created and maintained in being, so as to be carried beyond himself in responsible union with God in whom he finds his true life and felicity.

Of supreme importance here is the interwovenness of the knowledge of God and the knowledge of self, for therein consists man's life. Man is made to know God, so that he is not truly man unless he knows God. His whole manhood depends not only upon the grace of God in creation, but upon such a communication of His Word of grace that the image of God

[1] *Comm. on Gen.*, 2 : 9

123

becomes engraved, as Calvin said, on his person.[1] But we
do not know God truly unless we know that our knowing is
due to God alone; we must be able to trace the light back to its
source in God, realizing that in so doing we are brought into
immediate relation to the very fountain of Life. Otherwise
the light shines in the darkness, and the darkness comprehends
it not; but no man can be said to *live*, in the proper sense of the
word, in that condition. True knowledge involves in the very
act of knowing an acknowledgment that the Known is the
Master of our life and that we depend entirely upon His grace
in our being and knowing, and, as such, it carries with it a
profound knowledge of self. It is not that the knowledge of
self is in any sense a precondition of the knowledge of God,
but that the knowledge of God has not really come home to us
unless it has brought to us, in the realization of our utter
dependence on the grace of God, a true knowledge of our own
creaturehood. Therefore, we may say, man has been made in
such a way that he is not truly man except in the realization of
his creaturely dependence on the grace of God, and that he
cannot retain his life except in a motion of thankful acknowledgment of the sheer grace of God as Creator and Father in whose
Word man's life is deposited, and in the continuous communication of which alone may life be possessed. Nothing is more
characteristic of the whole of Reformed theology, and especially
of John Calvin, than this overwhelming sense of the grace of
God, and the note of unbounded thanksgiving as the true
life-answer of created man to the Father. The whole of the
Reformed doctrine of man is set forth in this context of grace
and thanksgiving.

It is in its teaching about the *imago dei* that Reformed
theology sets forth its doctrine of the creaturehood of man and
his relation to God; but that, in the nature of the case, can be
done only from the standpoint of the man renewed in Jesus
Christ. If man does not truly know himself until he knows God
truly, and until in that knowledge he becomes a true man, then
it is only from the standpoint of renewed man, face to face with
God in Christ, that we may understand the significance of the
fact that man is made in the image of God. Moreover, the

[1] *Comm. on Gen.*, Introd. Argument

coming of God in Christ, and His Self-communication to man, have taken such a form in the Incarnation, that it is there only that we may see human nature set forth in its truth as creature made to be the child of the heavenly Father. Thus there can be no question of trying to understand man out of himself, or from his relation to the world. He must be understood exclusively from the Word made flesh. It is as we behold the Word made flesh to be the glory of the only begotten of the Father, full of grace and truth, that we know not only that we are called to be the sons of God, but that our relation as sons to the Father rests, not on the will of man, but in faith on the will and power of God alone. The *imago dei* interpreted in this light carries the Reformed view of man.

Man is a creature in total dependence of being, and motion, and life, upon the gracious will of God. He is created out of nothing, and has neither origin nor being in himself, but is given being, and maintained in being, by the sheer grace of God. In relation to God, therefore, man is only an image. That is to say, his life is absolutely reflexive of the action of God, and can be lived only in a motion of continued reflexion. This is a very important point in the Reformed doctrine of man, for it is just here that a decisive break is made with the Aristotelian man of Scholastic theology, in which the living, dynamic relation of man to God is translated into a substantival and logical relation. Calvin was so firm upon this point that he would have nothing to do with secondary causation in theology, and inveighed against the tendency, becoming rampant in his own day, of speaking of *Nature* instead of *God*, thus *falsely transferring to nature what belongs to grace*.[1] Calvin's view of creation, and of the fallen world, was deeply Biblical and Hebraic in his insistence that everything created and worldly had to be related to the direct action of the gracious will of God. It was only after his day, when the mighty genius of Thomas Aquinas began to be felt, that the Reformed doctrine of man became hardened, and lost its essentially Reformed character. Then there came into being that strange amalgamation of Thomist logic and the Reformation view of man which came,

---

[1] *Inst.*, I, 5, 1; I, 16, 6; II, 2, 1, 27; *The True Method of Giving Peace and of Reforming the Church*, Calvin's *Tracts*, vol. 3, p. 242

unfortunately, to be known as "Calvinism". It is Karl Barth who has called Reformed theology back to its true position by insisting once again that we view man exclusively in the context of grace and the will of God in the sense of the Bible.

It is a mistake to think that Calvin believed in the primacy of the will, for he expressly repudiated the idea. On the other hand, he did not regard the will as an intellectual fiction, as it was apt to be regarded in the Aristotelian tradition. He gave it a significant place in his theology, and nowhere more so than in his doctrine of man. The creation was not just the utterance of a rational fiat upon the part of God, which then left created being with an existence in itself, even if it was a derived existence. He thought of creation as continuous and as continually depending on the communication of the divine Word, in such wise that it was maintained in being, and governed by immediate relation to the Will of God. Man is such a created being, body and soul, utterly dependent from moment to moment, though not in any atomistic fashion, upon the gracious will of God to create him, which refused to allow His original intention to be set aside even by the contradiction of sin. So closely did Calvin think of man's being as bound up with the will of God, that he said man would simply cease to exist if God were in any sense to withdraw His Spirit from him. Man depended from moment to moment on the grace of God as willing his existence. In this sense, Calvin used to think of man as being consumed and renewed every instant of his existence, for he was continuously being called out of non-being into being and life by the Word and will of the Creator, the Lord of life and death. Thus, the Spirit of God must be regarded as present to all existing things, maintaining them in existence, even in the case of the wicked and the reprobate. All creaturely endowments, such as wisdom, and craftsmanship, come directly as gifts from God, whether in the instance of unbelievers or of believers. All being and motion and life, wherever found, are due to the immediate action of the Spirit of God. Karl Barth has expressed this continual relation of the creature to the Creator very memorably in his teaching about the Holy Spirit. "The Holy Spirit is God Himself in so far as He is able, in an inconceivably real way, without being less God, to

be present to the creature, and in virtue of this presence of His
to realize the relation of the creature towards Himself, and in
virtue of this relation to vouchsafe life to the creature. The
creature requires the Creator in order to live. He thus requires
relation to Him. But this relation he cannot create. God creates
it through His presence to the creature, i.e., in the form of a
relation of Himself to Himself. The Spirit of God is God Himself
in His freedom to be present to the creature, and so to create
this relation, and thereby to be the life of the creature."[1]

That can be said of any living creature, but the distinctive
thing about man is that he was created in order to enjoy this
relation in a conscious and intelligent fashion. And so, according
to Calvin, man gets no profit from the presence of the Spirit
except through the Word;[2] but he was created to that very
end, with a special duty to give ear to the Word in which his
life was deposited,[3] and in the hearing and acknowledgment of
which he finds his true life as man, which is a life qualitatively
different from that of mere creaturehood. He is thus a creature
in the image of God, who knows that he is but a creature with
no life in himself, but who also knows that God has not only
called him into being, but has set His love upon him in order to
assume him into the divine fellowship as a child of the heavenly
Father. But as we may only worship God willingly, man can
retain his life in the Word only by a continuous thankful
acknowledgment of this gracious calling of God which carries
with it the confession of his creaturehood which is such that he
can presume upon nothing in himself, and arrogate nothing of
life or endowment to himself as if it were his own, and not the
sheer gift of God.[4] That is the meaning of *imago dei* in Reformed
theology. It is not a doctrine about man's being in himself,
but rather an acknowledgment that he depends entirely upon
the will of Another, whose grace and truth he images in a
knowledgable and obedient relation to the Word of Grace.
The *imago dei*, according to Calvin, consists essentially in the
objective act of grace by which God sets His love upon man, and
communicates to him, created with intelligence, His Word

---

[1] *The Doctrine of the Word of God*, pp. 515 f.
[2] *Inst.*, I, 9, 2 f.
[3] *Inst.*, I, 6, 2; I, 15, 6
[4] *Inst.*, II, 2, 1; II, 2, 10; *Comm. on Gen.*, 2:9; 3:6; *Serm. on Job*, 28:10 f.

accommodated to his creaturely capacity.[1] Thus the *imago dei* is grounded in the divine will to create man in fellowship with Himself, and that original intention remains, no matter what happens.[2] Were it not to remain, man would simply pass out of existence as man.

The objective basis of the *imago dei* lies, therefore, in the sheer grace of God. But man was made an intelligent being for fellowship with God in order that he might conform to the will and Word of God. This conformity of man is the imprinting of the *imago dei* on his person, as the Holy Spirit "with a wondrous and special energy forms the ear to hear, and the mind to understand" God.[3] And so the *imago dei* is the conscious but creaturely reflexion in man of the Word and grace of God— that is, the *imago dei*, in its subjective sense, is regarded as man's witness to the grace of God, and such a witness that the power and substance of it lie in the object witnessed to, and not in the witness itself. The strength of the *imago dei* and its continued maintenance in the believer lie in the Word of grace, and not in the soul. The *imago* has to do with man's being renewed in the spirit of his mind when it becomes formed to the Word by the *testimonium internum Spiritus Sancti*. In other words, it is lodged in man's thankful acknowledgment of God's sheer grace in setting His Fatherly favour upon him and choosing him to be a child of His love. But, as such, it is essentially a supernatural gift grounded in grace and possessed only in faith. It is not that which God has put into us by nature, but that which He has put into us by grace.[4] It has not first to do with our imaging God, but with God's beholding the work of His grace in us, and our consequent response to His beholding or His knowing of us, in thankfulness. Only thus can we image the glory of God, and only thus can we be men in the image of God.

This means that Reformed theology decisively repudiated the idea of St. Augustine that "in the mind itself, even before it is a partaker of God, His image is found".[5] In calling this Augustinian doctrine the discovery of antichrist, Karl Barth is

---

[1] *Comm. on Exod.*, 33: 19 f.; John, 5, 37; Rom. 1. 19; 1 Pet. 1, 22; *Inst.*, II, 6, 4
[2] *Comm. on Gen.*, 9 : 6   [3] *Inst.*, II, 2, 20 f.
[4] *Serm. on Job*, 10: 7 f., concluding prayer   [5] *De Trin.*, 14, 8

closely following in the steps of John Calvin and the Reformers who asserted that the attempt by man to take advantage of his imago-dependence on God, arrogating the image of God to himself as if it were a natural possession of his own being, was the very root motion of original sin suggested by the whisper of the serpent to our first parents. Ever since, said Calvin, this has continued to be the irrepressible source of all idolatry, for whatever man's reason conceives of God in this way is mere falsehood.[1] Once again this has become a living issue. What is at stake is the Biblical view of grace, and the Biblical account of the dynamic relation between man and God.

The next point to be discussed in any doctrine of man is the question of depravity. Here, again, Reformed theology starts from the fact of grace, and forms its judgment upon man's present depravity only as a corollary of the doctrine of grace. The revelation of the grace of God in Christ, which results in a new creation, carries with it a total judgment upon the natural man, including his mind and will. The fact that man must receive in faith his salvation, his true life, his righteousness, and wisdom, from outside of himself in Christ alone, carries with it the inference that, in himself, man has been utterly deprived of the *imago dei* wherein his life consists. That is the great Reformed inference from grace which forms the basis of the doctrine of sin. And it is just because faith must speak of salvation and forgiveness in total terms that it must also speak of sin and depravity in total terms. But it is only within the context of grace, and on the ground of grace, that we have any right to make such a total judgment upon man as he is—that is, it is only in the event of the new creation that we set aside the old man and all that pertains to him as having come under the total judgment of the Cross. It is important that this should be emphasized to-day, because the Reformed judgment on man's total depravity has been much misunderstood. Calvin himself often issued warnings against this sort of misunderstanding when he insisted that: "God does not delight in the degradation of man."[2] Apart from the judgment of grace there can be only an unhealthy knowledge of human depravity

---

[1] *Comm. on Exod.*, 32: 1
[2] *Comm. on Gen.*, 1: 26; cf. *on* 1 *Cor.*, 1: 31; *Inst.*, II, 2, 15; III, 2, 25

which is not only misanthropic but an insult to the Creator.[1] When grace is taken seriously it must be maintained that even the sinner who contradicts the grace of God is maintained in being by the same grace, while all his endowments and virtues are themselves directly due to the Spirit of God. The total judgment of grace, therefore, does not indicate a judgment upon these, in themselves, but means that they have been wholly polluted in the active perversity by which the sinner is mastered. Grace indicates that the whole relation between man and God, called the *imago dei*, has been perverted into its opposite, so that the truth of God is turned into a lie, and the glory of God into dishonour.[2]

This is a total judgment in the sense of the dynamic relation which Reformed theology thinks of as between man and God; but such a total judgment would be utterly impossible on the Scholastic view of man, and of evil defined as negation, and as involving necessarily privation of being. Total depravity does not entail on the Reformed view any ontological break in man's relation with God, but it does mean that the essential relation in which true human nature is grounded has been utterly perverted and turned into its opposite. Thus, it views "sin as properly of the mind",[3] and thinks of it as an active perversity which drags the whole man into pollution and inverts the whole order of creation. Sin is such a total affair that it suborns the good gifts of God, and indeed the whole man, who is maintained in being by the very grace of God, and directs man into an active relation of enmity to God. That is the astonishing revelation of sin which is given in the Gospel. By refusing to let man go, and therefore to fall back into non-being, the grace of God, in an event of inconceivable kindness, by holding on to its original intention for man, and by holding on to man himself, actually maintains him in the impossible existence of a sinner, in order at last to save him by the total judgment and forgiveness of God enacted in Christ Jesus and inserted into his life by the Cross.

[1] No one has spoken more forcibly on this view than Karl Barth: *Credo,* pp. 43 f.; *The Doctrine of the Word of God,* p. 466
[2] Calvin's expression is that the *imago Dei est tournée en son opprobre, Serm. on Job,* 33: 1 f.
[3] *Comm. on Rom.,* 2: 1; cf. *Serm on Eph.,* 2: 1 f.; 4: 17-26

This impossible situation of the sinner in active perversity against the will of God, and yet maintained in being by the mercy of God, is set forth in the doctrine of the Law. The Law indicates that God's original intention for man, which is the law of his being, is not dropped, but it is maintained in spite of the Fall of man. Now that he has fallen, however, it becomes man's judgment. That means that the *imago dei* was not dragged down by the Fall and made a prisoner of man's fallen nature, so that it might be manipulated by human thought or action within the abstraction of the world fallen from God; but it continues to hang over man as a destiny which he can realize no longer, and as a judgment upon his actual state of perversity. Wherefore, inasmuch as the *imago dei*, in the words of Calvin, is comprehended in the Law,[1] for God will not forgo His original intention any more than He will contradict His own glory for which He created man, we must treat our fellow men as made in the image of God, even though we see nothing in them but perversity. That we must do if we continue to acknowledge God's grace and creative intention toward man.

The very essence of sin, according to Calvin, is ingratitude. That is to say, instead of a thankful acknowledgment of God's grace, and of his utter creaturely dependence on it, wherein consists the *imago dei*, man has ungratefully presumed upon his relation to God, as made in God's image, and arrogated it to his own being. Sin, as the motion contradictory to grace, perverts man's relation to God into the exact contrary to the *imago dei*. Regarding the matter thus, Reformed theology cannot but talk in terms of total depravity or perversity, and, to be consistent, cannot talk about there remaining in fallen man, as such, any portion of the *imago dei*. If the *imago dei* is a dynamic *imago* corresponding to grace, then sin which is active perversity, utterly destroys the *imago dei* in man, though it cannot alter in one iota God's gracious intention by which man is still grasped in the hand of God. Fallen man is utterly corrupt inasmuch as he is mastered by the contradiction of sin, which, just because it opposes the grace of God, means the entire obliteration of the *imago dei* in man. No doubt he has been formed in God's image in the sense of *heritage*, but, now

---

[1] *Inst.*, III, 6, 1

that he is fallen, this *heritage* is not something that lies behind him and which can be passed on by human effort or by ancestral inheritance; rather does it lie in front of him as a destiny which he cannot achieve.[1] In other words, the fall of man means that the *imago dei* can be interpreted only in eschatological terms; certainly not in terms of natural inheritance, as if the grace of God could be bound to the perverted order of nature.[2] Thus, although God refuses to let go his original intention of grace enshrined in the conception of the *imago dei*, yet He "complains that the order appointed by Him has been so greatly disturbed that His own image has been transformed into flesh. . . . God gives the name of flesh as a mark of ignominy to men, whom He, nevertheless, had formed in His own image. . . . Indeed, the whole man is naturally flesh until by the grace of regeneration he begins to be spiritual."[3] "It was a sad and horrible spectacle that he in whom recently the glory of the divine image was shining, should lie hidden under fetid skins to cover his own disgrace, and that there should be more comeliness in a dead animal than in a living man!"[4]

Nevertheless, fallen man continues in his original sin—making more out of the *imago dei* than he ought. He continues to sin against the Word and Law of God in trying to lay hold upon the *imago dei* as comprehended in the Law and arrogating it to himself, thus turning himself into a thorough hypocrite by pretending that the Law of God is his own higher nature. This hypocrisy on the part of the carnal man, itself the very motion of sin, is devastatingly exposed at the Cross, where man finds that all efforts at self-justification are in enmity to God, and where justification by grace alone declares in no uncertain terms that fallen man is utterly destitute of *justitia originalis* or *imago dei*. It must be imputed by sheer grace. "Have we it through our own effort? Have we it by inheritance from our ancestors? No—but we have it by God's free gift through His own mere goodness."[5] Thus, the original intention of God becomes event in man's existence only by the Word, and the *imago* is possessed only in faith and hope until we see Christ

[1] *Comm. on Rom.*, 5: 12; *on* 1 *Cor.*, 15: 45; *Serm. on Job*, 14: 1 f.; 33: 1 f.; and 39, 8 f.
[2] *Comm. on Gen.*, 48: 17   [3] *Comm. on Gen.*, 6: 3
[4] *Comm. on Gen.*, 3: 22   [5] *Serm. on Job*, 33: 1 f.

as He is and become like Him. In Christ, therefore, we see the *Imago Dei* to be the ground of our existence beyond our existence, but which becomes sacramental event here and now in the hearing of faith, as we are sealed with the Holy Spirit until the redemption of the purchased possession.

We come now to the problem of natural theology, and here, too, it must be emphasized, Reformed theology takes its stand only within the inference from grace. When we come to know God in the Face of Jesus Christ, we know that we have not seen that Face elsewhere, and could not see it elsehow. Christ is the Way, the Truth, and the Life, and there is no door, nor way leading to the Father but by Him. And so the natural wisdom of the world about God is made foolishness at the Cross, and our natural knowledge is completely set aside by the new creation. Christ was not given to us, said Calvin, in order "to fill up or eke out our wisdom", but that "the accomplishment of the whole might be assigned exclusively to Him."[1] But that is known only in the actual event of grace, whereby man is made a new creature in Christ, so that old things are made to pass away, and all things become new.

Calvin laid great stress in discussing this question on the active perversity of the mind and the will, which he called *concupiscentia*. The very citadel of the mind, he said, had been seized by a sinful motion of pride and self-will, which was nothing else but sheer ingratitude and hostility to grace. Therefore every effort by the natural man to know God, even over against the evident tokens of God's grace manifested in the creation of the world, inevitably led him astray; so that, from the very first step, he was off the course, and, indeed, fighting against God. Thus natural theology can do nothing but move in a direction directly away from God, for, by every step it takes, it turns the truth of God into a lie.

In such a dynamic conception of man's relation to God as the Reformers envisaged, there are only two directions attributable to human existence: toward God, or away from Him; that is, in a direction corresponding to the motion of grace, or in a direction hostile to it. But grace reveals that the natural man in the very motion of his mind is enmity to God. He is unable

[1] *Comm. on* 1 *Cor.*, 1: 30; cf. *on Col.*, 2: 3

to know God, not only because he himself perverts the truth when it confronts him, but because God, who cannot be known against His will, that is, against His gracious Self-revelation, will not reveal Himself to human self-will and perversity. God does allow, said Calvin, enough light to reach man in his self-will to render him quite inexcusable (for even in disobedience there is an acknowledgment of God), but such that when, in a self-willed motion which refuses to surrender in thankfulness to grace, he attempts to make use of this to his own advantage, God blinds him and delivers him over to a reprobate mind. Reformed theology is quite clear upon the fact that no self-willed or self-propelled motion by unrepentant man can make the slightest progress toward knowing God. In fact, God has laid a curse upon natural knowledge, lest men should know Him and still remain in their perversity, so that now natural theology is in reality a bottomless pit in which a man is engulfed more and more in blindness and darkness. "If the light that is in thee be darkness, how great is that darkness." "The light of nature is stifled sooner than take the first step into this deadly abyss",[1] and so "the natural reason will never direct men to Christ."[2]

The position of Reformed theology in regard to man's knowledgable relation to God is exactly parallel to its position in regard to man's ontological relation to God. We noted above that Calvin, for example, thought of fallen man as maintained in being and maintained in being as a sinner, by the continuous creation of grace, else he would lapse back into sheer nothingness. Hence, we must think of all his natural endowments, reason, skill, etc., as maintained in being by the giving of grace. That means that grace reveals the sinner to have an inconceivable existence in grace itself, though that existence is over against the Law which becomes the challenge of grace accosting man in his sin and laying claim to him in his antagonism for God.

We must think of the natural man's knowledgable relation to God in the same way, as maintained in an impossible existence by the same action of grace, and yet as coming under the total judgment of grace in the event of the Cross and the

[1] *Inst.*, I, 2, 24; cf. I, 4, 1; *Comm. on 1 Pet.*, I: 21 [2] *Comm. on John*, I: 5

new creation in Christ. And so Calvin called natural religion a "shadow religion" over against the manifestation of God,[1] and Karl Barth, who has championed the Reformed rejection of natural theology to-day, has called it "the shadow-side" of the Revelation of God.[2] Barth has been seriously misunderstood here, but, in his essential position, he is not different from Calvin. He warns us, for example, that we have no right to deprive the natural man of his natural theology, for it is his only consolation in life and death, and, therefore, our rejection of natural theology must not be any kind of metaphysical denial; rather must it be grounded only upon the actual event of grace as setting it completely aside for faith.[3] There is no room whatever for it in a Christian theology, precisely because a Christian theology has to do with a new creation. But, in the event of this revelation, which is our new creation in Christ, we discover that even in our disobedience there was involved an acknowledgment of God, for it was only by God's Word that we were maintained in being as sinners against God. But, in the nature of the case, there is absolutely no road that way to God. There is only one road, by the Cross and the Resurrection of Jesus Christ whereby we are slain and made alive, but slain only in that we are made alive in Christ. The relevance of natural theology lies in the fact that God suspended His righteous judgment on man, and in that merciful suspension of His judgment kept man in being over against His Word, though in such a way that man could not realize his destiny of himself. But when God at last delivered His final judgment against sin and sinful existence, in the death of Christ, the apparent ground for a natural theology was destroyed, for the whole of natural man comes under the total judgment of the Cross. It was in the mercy of God, said St. Paul, that God suspended His total judgment until He prepared His new Creation; but just because that is the event by which the natural man with all his goodness and knowledge is slain, we have no right whatsoever to take up an attitude toward natural theology except within that event of grace. But within that event the Christian Church must stand by its own position in Christ, and refuse to build upon any other foundation than that

[1] *Inst.*, I, 4, 4   [2] *Dog.*, II, 1, p. 131   [3] *Op. cit.*, p. 190; cf. pp. 141 ff.

which was laid in Christ Jesus, the Self-revelation of God.

That alone is the ground for the Reformed polemic against the incursion of natural theology. It was on that ground, for example, that Karl Barth broke with Gogarten, in 1933, when the latter adopted a conception of the natural man in which his "nature" was not thought of as coming under the total action of Christ on the Cross, in judgment and new creation. It was then that Karl Barth became convinced that the vitality of natural theology is the vitality of the natural man, and that the whole question of natural theology is at stake in the Cross. Gogarten's position he held to be a complete betrayal of the Gospel, for it involved a reversal of the action of God in the death of Jesus Christ.[1] Gogarten wanted to base Christian theology upon the essential motion of the natural man, such that the Christian revelation perfects it and completes it. But that, said Barth, was the very motion of self-assertion and self-justification; in fact, the very motion which the grace of God in Christ contradicted on the Cross, and completely inverted. Therefore, now that the Cross has happened, we must forget the things which are behind, and begin again, laying no other foundation than that which has been laid in Christ Jesus. That is not to deny natural theology, as such, for that would mean a denial of the natural man in his actual existence, but it does mean that a Christian theology cannot be built upon a carnal foundation: to do that would be to open the flood-gates of naturalism and to inundate the Church with paganism. That that actually happened in Germany, in spite of Barth's warning, is evidence enough that the Christian Church is faced with a battle for its very existence in the issue of natural theology. To go back to the language of John Calvin: if the essential motion of sin is an unthankful and self-willed perversion of the gifts of God, then the divinely given "light of nature", and the "divinely deposited seed of religon" in man, can be nothing else in the activity of the natural man than the very "fountainhead of all superstition and idolatry"; and so we must regard natural religion as an "irreligious affectation of religion".[2] Once again the Church is faced with this pagan

---

[1] See the last number of *Zwischen den Zeiten*, and *Dog.*, II, 1, pp. 185 f.
[2] *Comm. on John*, 3: 6; cf. *on Psalm* 97: 7; *on Gen.*, 8: 21; *Inst.*, I, 5, 4, etc.

challenge mounted upon the irreligious affectation of religion whose roots go down to the light in the darkness of nature. The danger is, not that this should raise its head without the Church, but within it; and that, said Calvin long ago, can only be a "deadly abyss that swallows up all our thoughts".[1] The Reformer's point was that unless we regulate our knowledge carefully by the way in which God has willed that we shall know Him, then the perverted motion of our minds will only lead us into terrible darkness and confusion.

This perverted motion of man's mind Calvin described as the ungrateful attempt to turn the *imago dei* into something of man's own possession by the manipulation of which he could conceive a likeness of God. But, inasmuch as man possesses the *imago dei* only in a grateful response to the Word of grace, it is impossible for him to retain it in a motion of hostility to or alienation from the Word of grace. What man actually does in this perverted motion of the mind is to manipulate a wicked imagination, thus conceiving a dishonourable image of God which is a lie and not the truth. It is certainly true, said Calvin: that God cannot reveal Himself to us in any other way than by a comparison with things which we know. In His revelation God accommodates *Himself* in His Word to the capacity of our understanding, and in such a way that He not only makes Himself little, as it were, that we may grasp Him, but forms our ear to hear and shapes our minds to understand. Apart from that Self-accommodating motion of God's grace, we have no predisposition or faculty to know Him. Therefore, any attempt of theology which builds up a knowledge of God upon its own self-willed attempts to know God, not regulating its knowledge by the very activity of God's Word in and by which He fashions the only way in which we may know Him truly, can only invert the basic principles of Christian knowledge, and build up a false theology. "In order to know God, therefore, we must not frame a likeness of Him according to our own fancy, but we must betake ourselves to the Word, in which His lively image is exhibited to us. Satisfied with that communication, let us not attempt anything else of our own. . . . How ridiculous is the blindness of men when they claim anything for themselves;

[1] *Comm. on* 1 *Pet.,* 1: 21

for they gain by their boastings just as much as if some small creature, such as locusts, would elevate themselves by leaping; but they must immediately fall back upon the earth."[1] "It is hence evident", said Calvin again, "that men in vain weary themselves in serving God, except they observe the right way, and that all religions are not only vain, but also pernicious, *with which the true and certain knowledge of God is not connected.*"[2]

Once again, this position has been championed by Karl Barth, particularly in his discussion of the question of analogy by which he has worked out the Reformed teaching into a clear consistency. Barth makes no denial of analogy, as many English speaking theologians imagine.[3] Indeed it might be argued that the whole of his theological position is based on a vigorous affirmation of analogy, but it is an analogy of grace, not an analogy of being; therein is, Barth maintains, the great difference between the theology of the Reformers and that of the Schoolmen. There can be no doubt that all our knowledge of God is analogical, for we cannot know God except as human beings, and therefore only in analogical proportion to our human minds. Two things must be said, however, if this is to be understood aright.

(*a*) We must think of this analogy as dynamic and not static. That falls into line with the whole Reformed conception of man and his relation with God. In other words, Reformed theology has reinstated in the doctrine of analogy that essential moment of the will which had been left out, for example, in the doctrine of Thomas Aquinas. But the emphasis is first on the will of God, for it is God Himself who accommodates His Word to our understanding, and so it is God Himself who must preside in all our judgments about Him and about ourselves. This is what Barth has called the *analogia gratiae*, which is grounded essentially on the Incarnation, for it is there that God in definitive fashion accommodates His Word to our knowing. If therefore there is a true analogy of proportionality, as the Thomists aver, it must be one grounded, not on any abstractly conceived ontological continuity between man and God, but on the *unio hypostatica* in which we have the union of God

---

[1] *Comm. on Isa.*, 40: 19 f.
[2] *Comm. on Heb.*, 11: 6; cf. *on* 1 *Cor.*, 2: 12
[3] e.g., R. Niebuhr, *The Nature and Destiny of Man*, Vol. 2, p. 69

and man as God Himself has set it forth in Christ, and in which we may be united to God by partaking of that union in faith. We cannot, therefore, set forth a doctrine of the image of God or of analogy already lodged in the being of man, as Augustine taught, before men are partakers of God. Thus, the true analogy of proportionality grounded upon the Word and grace of God will be set forth in this fashion: man and God are related in the mutual relation of faith and grace *proportionaliter* to the relation of Man and God in hypostatic union in Christ Jesus. That means that a Christian doctrine of the Word of God and human decision, of election and human faith, of the Divine Presence and the worldly element in the sacrament, etc., will be grounded entirely upon the hypostatic union as its true and only valid analogy; that is, upon the central relation and union of God and Man of which every other relation must partake.

The fundamental mistake in a doctrine of analogy is to turn the dynamic analogy into a static analogy of being. That may be done by converting the dynamic relation into a logical (ontic-noetic) relation, or/and by a view of grace as a transferable quality infused into and adhering in finite being so as to raise it to a different gradation where it can grasp God by a connatural proportion of being. Both these activities are repudiated by Reformed theology as unbiblical, unchristian, and fictional. Reformed theology goes a step farther, and points out that the desire to stabilize the analogy, or to transubstantiate it into an analogy of being, so that it can be humanly manipulated at will, belongs to the very essence of sin and human pride by which our first parents fell. It is the desire by man to possess likeness to God in the continuity of space and time secure at every moment in his own hand and being, instead of being ready to live in the acknowledgment that his life is deposited only in the Word of God, and may be retained only by acknowledgment that it is not his own but belongs to God, and is only his by continual communication through the Word of grace.

(b) From man's side, the analogy must correspond with the essential motion of grace. That is to say, the analogy cannot be possessed by man or used except in a motion that is correlative to the motion of sheer grace. No analogy grounded upon the self-asserting or self-explanation of man, or partaking of self-will, will pass the required test and correspond with the downward movement of grace. In Calvin's view, a true motion corresponding with this analogy of grace is the self-emptying of faith, and the acknowledgment of thankfulness which carries man out beyond himself to depend entirely upon the movement of grace. To grasp the grace of God in such a way as to do justice to grace, man must stretch out an empty hand. Thus, the motion corresponding to grace entails on the part of man a downward or a humble movement; not a movement of self-assertion, as if by an *analogia entis* he would or could add one cubit to his stature. The true movement of grace, Reformed theology holds, is impugned by a doctrine of *analogia entis*. By the entry of sin, the true analogy of grace has been inverted; and that perverted or inverted activity, said Calvin, never ceases, so long as we are unredeemed. But all our natural theology is built upon this inverted analogy of grace, so that we indulge in a "wicked exercise of the understanding that always contrives in what way it may rob God of the praise which is His due".[1] It is that active perversity, or the inversion of grace, that constitutes the difficulty for theology, for, whenever the Word of grace confronts us in Christ, the inverted analogy must be re-inverted, and restored to its truth in the motion of grace.

The Incarnation, as culminating in the Cross and the Resurrection, is the great act of God in which He entered our perverted order of nature, and wrought the basic soteriological inversion by which we are reconciled to God. But that basic soteriological inversion must be pushed through the whole region of the mind, inasmuch as we are alienated from God, as Calvin said, "in the whole of our mental system."[2] Therefore "let this mind be in you, which was also in Christ Jesus. . . ." That takes place in the Christian *metanoia*, when the believer transformed by the renewing of his mind, knows that he has not chosen Christ, but that Christ has chosen him; that his knowing of God is grounded on his being known of God; and

---

[1] *Comm. on Isaiah*, 48: 5
[2] *Comm. on Col.*, 1: 21; cf. 1 *Cor.*, 1: 21; *Inst.*, II, 15, 9

that every analogy of men, such as fatherhood, is grounded reflexively upon the action and love of the heavenly Father, after whom every fatherhood in heaven and earth is named. Unless theological activity is grounded upon, and made to conform to, this motion of grace, then every step of theology can only be from alienation to alienation in the continued assertion of self-will; instead of from faith to faith, in the continued receiving of grace for grace, in which the true life of man consists. The Christian revelation discovers to us that our existence is grace through and through, but also grace in a special sense: that we have been so made, as intelligent beings, that we must give an intelligent life-answer to grace in such a way that our existence is ours only as we re-live our grace-existence in a thankful and knowledgable motion in answer to the Word of grace. Therefore, there can be no true *ordo cognoscendi* (order of knowing) which is not based upon an *ordo essendi* (order of being) conceived entirely as grace, and the *ordo essendi* reaches its true destiny in the *ordo cognoscendi*. This is the problem of analogy as Reformed theology sees it to-day. The *analogia entis* is entirely grounded upon the *analogia gratiae*, and only in an *analogia fidei* corresponding to the *analogia gratiae* does the *analogia entis* have any truth or reality.[1] Outside of that, the truth of God is inevitably turned into a lie.

For this reason, Reformed theology is grounded upon the "mutual relation of faith and grace" through the Word.[2] It is the Word, the lively and essential Image of God, which is the *analogia analogans*, so that only over against its activity does man have an *analogia analogata*: that is to say, an *analogia fidei* corresponding with an *analogia gratiae*,[3] that we may know God truly, and, in that knowledge, truly be what God meant us to be, men in the image of God.

[1] It is interesting to find Franciscan theology attempting to make a similar movement to-day. Thus Gottlieb Söhngen insists that the *analogia entis* must be subordinated to the *analogia fidei*, on the principle that *esse sequitur operari*, and not *vice versa*: *Catholica*, 1934, vol. 4, pp. 97 f.; cf. vol. 3, pp. 10 f.; and also *Wissenschaft u. Weisheit*, 2, Jahrg., pp. 97 f.
[2] *Comm. on Acts*, 15, 9
[3] Cf. *Dog.*, II, 1, pp. 86 ff. and 267 ff.

III

THE REDISCOVERY OF THE BIBLE

By G. HENDRY, B.D.

THE last quarter of a century has witnessed the beginnings of a remarkable transformation in the field of Bible study. In this period it has come to a point which may be compared with that of Christian in *The Pilgrim's Progress*, when, having rested awhile in the pleasant arbor "about the midway to the top of the Hill Difficulty" and then proceeding on his way, "he felt in his bosom for his Roll, that he might read therein and be comforted; but he felt and found it not"; whereupon he resolved to go back and search "if happily he might find his Roll, that had been his comfort so many times in his Journey". During the first two decades of the century, roughly to the period of the first world-war, Biblical study was still dominated by the critical interest; its energies were devoted to the sifting of the text, the analysis of the documents, the tracing of the sources, and the illumination of the historical and cultural background— all necessary work—this is the Hill Difficulty which cannot be evaded; for the Bible is, on the face of it, a collection of human documents, and no attempt to understand it which ignores the fact can hope to be successful. But towards the close of the First World War[1] it began to be felt that all was not well; that for all the success which criticism had achieved in breasting the Hill Difficulty with the formidable scientific equipment it had acquired, something was amiss: Christian missed his Roll. It is significant that the loss made itself felt first, not to the scholar but to the preacher, who, face to face with "the hungry sheep" that looked up and sought to be fed, became painfully aware that the rations issued by critical scholarship afforded a miserably inadequate *ersatz* diet.[2] In his distress the preacher was driven to search the Scriptures anew to see if the missing

---

[1] Wellhausen died in 1918; Barth's *Romans* made its first appearance in 1918
[2] Barth: *Not und Verheissung der christlichen Verkündigung*, 1922

Roll had been lost irretrievably or perchance only buried under the excavations which the critical engineers had made in the side of the Hill.

This is the historical starting-point of the so-called "theology of crisis". It arose out of the real, practical crisis of the preacher facing the problem: What is the Word of God in the Bible? In reopening this problem, Barth recalled theology to its essential task, and it is apparent that his call has been heard far beyond the confines of those who profess and call themselves Barthians. No one who compares the main trend of Biblical study to-day with that of twenty-five years ago can fail to note the change of emphasis. Whereas, then, broadly speaking, the general endeavour was to seek what light could be shed upon the Bible by literary, historical, archaeological research, to-day there is a new disposition to seek what light the Bible has to shed upon us. Critical study has indeed gone on—and let us hope that it will continue to shed further light upon the Bible —but there is manifest on all hands to-day a new concern to find out what, after all, the Bible means, what its own authentic message is, and to recover the theological interpretation of the Bible as the word of God.[1]

There can be no doubt that it was Barth's challenge which gave the decisive impulse to this movement.[2] His first work, which was written with the zest of one who had made a discovery,[3] was interpreted in some quarters as an attack upon criticism and an attempt to resuscitate the older "orthodox" view of Scripture; he speaks humorously of having to defend himself against the charge of seeking to institute a "Diocletian persecution" of criticism. But the truth is that he was no longer moving on the lines of the old antithesis of fundamentalism and modernism and had advanced a decisive step beyond it towards the synthesis (if we may employ the Hegelian scheme). Barth did not dispute the right of the application of the critical method to the study of the Bible; he only challenged the

[1] See the essay by John Lowe on "The Recovery of the Theological Interpretation of the Bible" in the volume, *The Interpretation of the Bible*, edited by C. W. Dugmore, 1944
[2] To speak of "the rediscovery of the Bible" (the title is not of my choosing) is to exaggerate; for the Bible has never been completely lost, as Barth himself acknowledges. *Dog.*, I, 2, p. 508
[3] Preface to the first edition of *Romans*

pretension of criticism to deliver the authentic message of the Bible. He saw that, even when criticism had done its work, the real task of interpreting the Bible remained to be done: criticism could help to prepare the way and to erect the scaffolding for this task, but it could not itself discharge it. The significance of Barth's work is that it brought theology from the critical to the post-critical phase of Bible study, or, as we may say, from adolescence to maturity.

How is the Bible to be read in order to be understood aright? We must seek the answer to this question in the Bible itself, first of all; in a humble and patient endeavour to listen to what the Bible says of itself and to understand it as it understands itself. Until this is done, the question of the truth of the Bible cannot properly be raised. There is no suggestion that this question is to be evaded, and that we have to bow in blind submission before the authority of the Bible. The Bible itself calls for decision. Only, it is essential that the decision should be made on what the Bible really says of itself, and not on what has been read out of it, or into it, with the help of some preconceived theory. Even a positive decision in favour of the truth or "value" of the Bible is a decision against it when it is reached by a denial or distortion of the Bible's testimony concerning itself.

What, then, is the Bible? The Bible itself gives the answer: that it is a book of the words of men which bear witness to the Word of God and which are, therefore, the Word of God. In this book men bear witness that God has spoken to them and through them.

If there is anything to which the name of "rediscovery" may be applied, it is surely to this view of the Bible (which is but the Bible's view of itself) as *witness* to the Word of God. It liberates us from the false antithesis which had been set up by "orthodoxy" and "liberalism", through each concentrating its attention on one aspect of the Bible, to the detriment of the other, and enables us to see it in both its aspects, without detriment to either.

When we understand the Bible as witness to the Word of God, we recognize that it consists of the words of men, the words of Moses, David, Isaiah, Mark, John, Paul, and the rest. There

convince us that they faithfully delivered the oracles which were divinely entrusted to them. . . . The Scripture . . . ought not to be made the subject of demonstration and arguments from reason; but it obtains the credit which it deserves with us by the testimony of the Spirit. For, though it procures our respect by its inherent majesty, it never seriously affects us till it is confirmed by the Spirit in our hearts."[1] The Reformed doctrine of the *testimonium Spiritus Sancti* remained at least a formal check against any confusion of the issues, even after the fantastic idea of verbal inerrancy had established itself. It is instructive to observe how carefully the authors of the Westminster Confession distinguish between the intrinsic authority of the Word of God and the excellence or value of the Bible, even though they had "so high and reverent esteem for the Holy Scripture" that they could speak, uncritically, of "the entire perfection thereof".

> The authority of the Holy Scripture, for which it ought to be believed and obeyed, dependeth not upon the testimony of any man or Church, but wholly upon God (who is truth itself), the author thereof; and therefore it is to be received because it is the word of God. We may be moved and induced by the testimony of the Church to an high and reverent esteem for the Holy Scripture; and the heavenliness of the matter, the efficacy of the doctrine, the majesty of the style, the consent of all the parts, the scope of the whole (which is to give all glory to God), the full discovery it makes of the only way of man's salvation, the many other incomparable excellencies, and the entire perfection thereof, are arguments whereby it doth abundantly evidence itself to be the word of God; yet, notwithstanding, our full persuasion of the infallible truth, and divine authority thereof, is from the inward work of the Holy Spirit, bearing witness by and with the word in our hearts.[2]

The question whether we read the Bible critically or uncritically is certainly important, but it must not be confused with the question how the Bible is to be received as the Word of God.

When we observe this distinction, we are sometimes asked what, then, we mean by divine revelation, and how it authenticates itself; and it is held against us that we are unable to give

---

[1] *Inst.*, I, 7, 4   [2] c. I, 4, 5

a satisfactory answer.[1] But how should we? If we could explain what divine revelation is, and how it is possible, what we explained would be precisely not divine revelation. We may not pretend to usurp the office of the Holy Spirit. The Word of God, if it means anything at all, means something different from the words of men: it is the Word before which man occupies essentially the position of hearer, in contrast to all the words of which he is or can be the speaker. How should his own speaking, even though he spoke with the tongues of men and of angels, become identical with the Word of God? To speak of the Word of God, when all that is meant is the words of men raised to the nth degree, is an abuse of language. If the Word of God is the Word of which God is the speaker, how could it be authenticated by any but God Himself? We can, and indeed it is our bounden duty to, testify by our words and our actions that we have heard the Word of God, but nothing that we can say or do can authenticate it. To seek to prove here would only be to disprove.

Are we, then, left suspended in a void? Much of the difficulty and confusion that surrounds the problem of the Bible arises from the fact that the problem is erroneously posed in a void. It is important to realize, as Barth has pointed out, that the problem of the Bible as the Word of God is in fact posed and can only be posed within the Church. It is the Church's confession of faith in the Bible as the Word of God which raises the problem. How did any of us come to entertain the notion that this book is the Word of God? It would be gross conceit on our part to pretend that we had come to it by independent study and research. We came to it because we were first told that it is

[1] Matthews, *God in Christian Thought and Experience*, Preface to Fifth Edition; Lowe, *op. cit.* The strictures of Lowe on "the dialectical neo-Calvinism which exalts the word of God into a slogan at the cost of completely obscuring what the word of God is" show that he has failed to grasp the point of neo-Calvinism, which is, that the word of God is the word *of God*. On the other hand, a distinguished philosopher, who died recently, has written these as his last words: "I would have those of us who are in danger of imagining themselves to be an élite to remember how it is written that the secret of the Lord is neither with the mighty, nor with the learned and ingenious, but with 'them that fear Him', and that it has pleased Him to use 'the foolishness of preaching' to confound the wisdom of this world. Our own society has long been drifting dangerously towards spiritual death because it has chosen to think otherwise; if its malady is to be healed, we shall need once more to take the thought of actual *revelation* from God more seriously than some of us have been wont to do. . . ." (A. E. Taylor, *Does God Exist?* p. 171)

the Word of God by those who were before us in the Church. It is not the case that we lighted upon a collection of ancient documents which we proceeded to read, study, examine, and analyse in order to see what we could make of them; the Bible was *given* into our hands and we were *told* that it is the Word of God. This does not excuse us from the duty of reading the Bible for ourselves and seeking the Word of God according to the testimony of the Church. But that is a very different thing from discounting the testimony of the Church at the outset and approaching the Bible in "the spirit of independent scientific enquiry". The fundamental error of modern criticism is that, while it brought in all manner of witnesses, literary, historical, archaeological, philological, and the rest, to assist it in examining the case of the Bible, it failed to examine the principal witness, and took no account of the special character of his testimony. It severed the Bible from the context in which it was received as the Word of God, and proceeded on the assumption that it could establish the conclusion by "independent" enquiry; which means, in fact, on the basis of presuppositions other than that on which the confession that the Bible is the Word of God rests. It proposed to play *Hamlet* without the Prince of Denmark, and it is small wonder that this procedure should issue in the attempt to ascribe the rôle to Polonius.

We are bound in the first place to listen to the judgment of the Church concerning the Bible. We do not have to obey it, but we have certainly to pay attention to it and examine it; for the judgment of the Church is expressed in its confession of *faith.* The Church's acceptance and recognition of the Bible as the Word of God is not the conclusion of a syllogism (for where could it find the premisses?); it is an act of faith and obedience. We have no *tertium comparationis* by which we could prove the judgment of the Church that the Bible is the Word of God. The testimony of the Church is that we can only prove that the Bible is the Word of God when it proves itself by evoking the same testimony of faith and obedience in ourselves.

When we read the Bible as a human document, and when we take its human character quite seriously, we have to recognize that it points beyond itself to an object. Therefore, we understand it aright only when our attention is drawn beyond the human words themselves and directed to the object to which they point. This applies equally to the Bible and to all human words. But it is peculiar to the object, to which the human words of the Bible point, that it can only make itself known by itself; it is not within their power to bring it on the stage; for it is the Word of God, and the Word of God can only be spoken by God Himself.[1] The human voices of the Bible bear witness that they have heard the Word of God and that they expect to hear it again; but between this recollection and this expectation there is a gap, an empty place, which they cannot fill and which can be filled only by the living voice of God Himself.[2]

But, while we must distinguish between the Bible and the Word of God to which it bears witness, we cannot separate them. We cannot penetrate behind the words of the Bible and obtain a view of the facts or realities independently of them. We cannot look over the shoulders of the prophets and apostles and see what they saw better and more clearly than they saw it. The form and content of the Bible, though distinguishable, are inseparable. The Word of God comes to us only in the form of the testimony of the prophets and apostles who were the first and chosen witnesses of revelation. It is the only testimony to it that we have, and we cannot discard it and place ourselves in a direct relation to revelation. We are bound to the Bible. Thus it is proper to say that the Bible is the Word of God. The witness of prophets and apostles is bound up with the singleness and contingency of revelation. We have, so far as is at present known, no other writings of which this can be said, and therefore the Bible occupies a special position in the Church as canonical, holy Scripture.

An objection which is frequently brought against this doctrine is that it unduly narrows the field of divine revelation. Why should revelation be confined to the Bible? Proposals are made for extending it by recognizing additional fields of divine revelation in nature and history and in the non-Christian religions. Dr. Matthews expresses his criticism thus: "The real difference between us is not that Barth believes in revelation and I do not, but that my view of revelation is wider than his. I cannot confine revelation to the Bible nor do I suppose that

[1] *Dog.*, I, 2, p. 519   [2] p. 534

God has left Himself without witness in any time or place. Any conception of revelation which would completely sever Christianity from the rest of the religious experience of mankind would be to me historically impossible and theologically false ... Do they [Barth and those who agree with him] assert that revelation is wholly absent from all religions except Christianity?"[1] In order to be able to answer this question, we should require to have at our disposal a general "conception" or theory of revelation which we could apply as a kind of yardstick to the religious experience of mankind and so determine where revelation is present and where it is not. But, if we could obtain such a general conception of revelation—and it is difficult to see whence it could be derived and whether it would have any real meaning—it would be inapplicable to the Bible, which understands itself, not as a particular instance of a general law, but as witness to a single, contingent event. We know revelation only in the form in which it meets us in the Bible; and the form is inseparable from the content, as the humanity of Jesus Christ is inseparable from His divinity. To make free with a general conception of revelation and to apply it critically to "the religious experience of mankind" implies the possession of something which we do not have and in the nature of the case could not have. "Revelation is the subject of the Biblical testimony. But we have no testimony to it except this. And thus we have no points of comparison which could enable us to liberate ourselves, even partially, from this testimony, and place ourselves in a direct relation to its subject."[2]

To state the issue in a more concrete form: the central fact of divine revelation to which the Bible bears witness is the person of Jesus Christ. Is there anything in the rest of the religious experience of mankind or among the phenomena of nature of which it can be affirmed, as of the Scriptures, that they testify of Him, and that they are able to make us wise unto salvation through faith which is in Christ Jesus?

The Bible is the Word of God. But when we say this, we must not forget that the reality of this "is" rests upon a divine and not upon a human possibility. It is a divine choice and a divine decision. We cannot prove that the Bible is the Word of

---

[1] Matthews, *loc. cit.*   [2] *Dog.*, I, 2, p. 545

God; we cannot point to some quality inherent in the Bible from which we could draw this conclusion. It would perhaps be truer to say that the Bible becomes the Word of God; it becomes the Word of God when it overpowers us and gains the mastery over us,[1] i.e., when it creates faith in us. When the Word of God creates faith in us, this is God's own work, His miracle, His in-Spirit-ing. It is not in our power to make it happen. At the best we can pray for it.[2] This, in all its simplicity, is the doctrine of the inspiration of the Bible. The door of the Bible can be opened only from within.

The reader may feel that the title of this essay calls for some more practical and concrete justification, and he may ask whether Barth's restatement of the evangelical doctrine of Scripture has in fact helped towards a better understanding of the Bible. The proof of the pudding is the eating of it; and the test of a doctrine of Scripture is the measure in which it enables us to listen to what the Bible itself says. "The doctrine of Scripture is nothing but the necessary index of its right exposition; it can claim no abstract validity for itself but must obtain its confirmation in actual exposition."[3] It may fittingly be asked, therefore, whether this doctrine has had a fructifying effect on the field of exegesis.

Space permits of attention being drawn to one feature only of some recent Biblical exposition which is striking and suggestive, and that is the evidence of a new concern to grasp the unity of the Bible. The general effect of the labours of criticism had been to disintegrate the Bible, to break it up into a number of parts with little or no real connection between them. There was an inclination to drive a wedge between the Gospels and the Epistles, and to deepen this into an antithesis between "the religion of Jesus" and "the faith of Paul". Further, "the quest of the historical Jesus" led to a separating of the Synoptics from the Fourth Gospel and a disparagement of the "historical" value of the latter. Above all, there was a tendency to dig a deep gulf between the Old Testament and the New Testament and to represent the Old Testament as of minor significance for the faith of Christ, or even as completely

[1] "bemächtigt", Dog., I, 2, p. 561
[2] op. cit., 590. Barth compares the Bible to the water of the Pool of Bethesda
[3] Dog., I, 2, p. 511

negligible. Harnack resuscitated Marcion's demand for the removal of the Old Testament from the Canon of Christian Scriptures; and some eclectics have advocated its replacement by the sacred books of the world-religions. Even when critics of a more conservative disposition proclaimed the abiding value of the Old Testament, the underlying assumption was that the labours of criticism had destroyed the authority of the Old Testament; and they gave the impression of seeking salvage among the ruins.

Now, the Bible is given into our hands as a single volume, and this is no accident but the outward sign of the Church's confession of faith, as expressed in the Canon, that the various writings contained in this volume bear a single and united testimony to the Word of God. The Canon imposes upon us the task of endeavouring to understand the Bible as a unity. An interpretation of the Bible which, while recognizing the diversity of its component parts, leads towards a view of its unity is *prima facie* better than one which magnifies the diversity; thus, for instance, if we are able to understand Paul and James as intending the same thing, the presumption is that we understand each of them better than when we see them only as irreconcilably opposed. The question is whether such an understanding can be attained by genuine exposition of the text, and not by an arbitrary imposition.

It is well to be clear about what is involved here. In spite of the strong prejudice against reading anything *into* the Bible as "unscientific" and "obscurantist", it may fairly be maintained that no one can read anything at all out of the Bible without at the same time reading something into it. How, indeed, could we understand the Bible at all unless we had some notion of the meaning of the words with which it addresses us; and how can we be certain that the meanings we attach to the words correspond exactly to the sense of the Bible? The idea that it is possible to approach the Bible (or any subject of knowledge) in a "scientific" spirit with a mind free of all presuppositions, a *tabula rasa*, is an exploded myth.[1] We should

---

[1] This was acknowledged by a leading Old Testament scholar, Professor Johannes Hempel, in his presidential address to the second international congress of O.T. scholars at Göttingen in September, 1935, according to the report in *Theologische Blätter*, 1935, col. 235

do well to emulate the humility of the Ethiopian eunuch who, when asked: "Understandest thou what thou readest?" replied: "How can I, except some man should guide me?" (Acts 8: 31). Such guidance would not be so necessary if the subject of the Bible were present in it in such a way that it could be obtained by patient study of the text. But the subject of the Bible is God's revelation of Himself, and it is present in the Bible only in the sense that the Bible bears witness to it. The Bible record is of the recollection and expectation of God's revelation; but the reality of revelation at the meeting-point is not "contained" in the Bible. It is God's own prerogative. It is present in the Bible only as the centre round which the testimony of the Bible turns; it stands at the vanishing-point of the Biblical perspectives. It is this hidden centre which gives the Bible its unity; its unity is not inherent in itself, and thus it cannot be demonstrated or systematized in the form of a unified Biblical *Weltanschauung*. But while the unity of the Bible can be no more than a presupposition of exegesis, an exegesis which is able to attain to an approximate confirmation of it is truer than one which recedes from it.

Some notable advances have been made in the direction of such an exegesis within recent decades. The form-historical study of the Gospels has done much to close the breach which liberal criticism had made between the "simple history" narrated in the Synoptics and the "doctrinal superstructure" erected upon it in the Fourth Gospel and the Epistles, by showing that the peculiar form in which the history of Jesus is narrated corresponds to the faith of the Lord Jesus Christ which is doctrinally set forth in the Epistles. It is the same faith which *in-forms* both. A more striking, because more necessary, advance in the direction of the unity of the Bible is seen in the new endeavours to reach a theological, or rather a Christological, interpretation of the Old Testament. The results of literary and historical criticism had seemed to leave no room for any but a genealogical interpretation; and the retention of the Old Testament in the *corpus* of Scripture was justified only by invoking the idea of progressive revelation. The facts that the Old Testament is an historical record; that, like all such, it is a record of growth and change; and that we can trace in it the gradual evolution of man's apprehension of God—these are facts which have been established by modern criticism; the marvel is only that they were so late in being discovered. But the invocation of the idea of progressive revelation to account for them, natural enough in view of the prevailing intellectual atmosphere of the nineteenth century, is a different matter. This attempt to translate theology into terms of biology involves serious difficulties. If this theory is a true account of revelation, it is difficult to see how the earlier stages, which, *ex hypothesi*, we have in the Old Testament, can have any other than an antiquarian interest for us, as Stephenson's Rocket has for the railway traveller of to-day. Further, the implied view of revelation as a process of education is intellectualistic and academic, and it leaves the position of those who did not survive the kindergarten stage somewhat obscure. But, above all, it misconceives the real subject of the Bible, which is not man's apprehension of God, but God's apprehension of man. We may certainly trace a development in man's apprehension of God, or, at all events, in his attempts to express his apprehension of God; but it by no means follows that we can speak of a corresponding development in God's apprehension of man; that is an inference to which the Bible lends no countenance. Revelation is an act of God's initiative, and it is not to be wondered at that man's recognition and response should be laggard and should show varying degrees of more and less; in point of fact, it is regress that the Bible speaks of for the most part: the Old Testament understands itself as a record of retrogression.[1]

The existence of a new concern with the theological interpretation of the Old Testament is attested by a number of recent publications, such as *The Throne of David* by A. G. Hebert. But the most notable endeavour to "reverse the inversion" which was brought about by the application of the evolutionary theory to the Old Testament is to be seen in the work of Wilhelm Vischer. It is not possible in the space available to do more than direct attention to Vischer's work—some

[1] It will be remembered that Paul, who was of those "upon whom the ends of the world were come" (1 Cor. 10: 11), still counted himself not to have apprehended (Phil. 3: 13)

account of it has been given by the present writer elsewhere.[1]
Suffice it to say here that, if we may truly speak of a "rediscovery of the Bible", Vischer's volumes on "The Witness of
the Old Testament to Christ"[2] form the greatest single contribution to it, and they represent the boldest advance yet
made in the direction indicated by Barth when he says: "The
real decision whether we are moving towards better things in
this field will depend on whether . . . the time of more or less
arbitrarily selected themes is over, and the exegesis of canonical
Scripture, i.e., the connected exposition of Genesis, Isaiah,
Matthew, etc., in their actually existing form and volume, is
again recognized as the only possible goal of Biblical science
and undertaken anew."[3]

[1] In an article entitled, "The Old Testament in the Christian Church", in
Crisis Christology, Dubuque, Iowa, 1945, Vol. 3
[2] *Das Christuszeugnis des Alten Testaments. Bd.* I (*das Gesetz*), Munich, 1935;
Bd. II (*die früheren Propheten*), Zollikon-Züich, 1942
[3] *Dog.*, I, 2, p. 547

THE FAITH THAT SAVES

By H. F. LOVELL COCKS, M.A., D.D.

(1)

WHAT is saving faith? *Saving faith is the sinner's acknowledgment of the living God who encounters him in His Word.* It is man's trustful, obedient response to divine grace; the human act that is "conformed" to God's act of self-revelation.

The term *saving faith* does indeed suggest a contrast with faith of some other kind, and there is obviously a belief in God that under many diverse forms is universal in human experience. Religion is a perennial human concern. There is a characteristic urge in our human reason that drives us beyond the evidence of our senses and impels us to affirm the reality of the supernatural and the existence of a Being of almighty power and transcendent goodness. Moreover, this venture into the Unknown, this believing in advance of evidence and even against it, is not only the nerve of religion, in the more usual interpretation of that word, but the foundation of scientific discovery, artistic intuition and creation, and of the entire forward-looking, practical enterprise of everyday living. It is tempting to think that here, at the very roots of human experience, we have found that faith in God which comes to full self-consciousness in the "saving faith" of the Christian believer. The identification of this natural faith with the faith that saves seems to provide us with a triumphant apologetic. To the attacks of scientific humanists and materialistic philosophers we can reply by pointing out that even the scientist must live and work by faith. We can say that "faith is the presupposition of all discovery and of all progress in knowledge"; that "all men live by deep, inexorable intuitions, such as that of the plain man who trusts to common sense, that of the physicist who makes use of unprovable hypothesis, and that of the religious man whose faith is response to revelation."[1]

[1] J. S. Whale, *Christian Doctrine*, p. 27

That man lives by faith in this sense of the word is not to be denied, but when this *natural faith*, as we may call it, is identified with the saving faith of the Christian believer, we have made a false start and are heading for a complete misunderstanding, not only of saving faith, but also of revelation. In fact, this identification is possible only because revelation has already been misunderstood. Saving faith is linked to the Word; the human response is matched to the divine initiative. And, as we shall see, misconceptions regarding the nature of the Word produce analogous misconceptions of faith.

The apologists who make much of the alleged continuity between natural faith and saving faith are always telling us that faith is an act of the whole man. For them, this means not only that the misguided attempt to locate faith in some specific religious sense is to be abandoned, but that faith is to be seen as the sum of man's rational powers in their most vigorous and harmonious exercise. Here, if anywhere—so their argument runs—we see man as he is, reaching out in his religious need towards a universe which, so far as it is rational, must meet that need and reward man's aspiring spirit with the satisfactions it craves. Thus, on the foundation of man's inextinguishable religiousness, of his "wholeness" in faith, we may postulate the wholeness of Reality. Thus we vindicate religious experience and prove the existence of God.

Now we agree, and even insist, that faith[1] is the act of the whole man. But, for us, this does not mean that we can take faith for granted and pass on to our apologetic task; but that faith itself becomes our problem. For where is this "whole man" to be found? Is man as we know him a whole man? No one denies that psychologically he is a whole—that his every act of believing or knowing or willing is a harmony of the cognitive, affective and volitional elements of his psychical nature. Again, no one denies that he is an epistemological whole—that in his knowing he is, and may know himself to be, a unity over against the object of his knowing. But these psychological and epistemological unities are quite irrelevant here. Where is man a moral and spiritual unity?—that is the question. Certainly not in his religion. For, if religion means

[1] From this point "faith" means "saving faith"

man's inescapable consciousness of the unseen, supernatural world, and his attempts to relate his existence to that world and to quieten his uneasy conscience by ritual observances and "good works", then, so far from being an expression of his moral and spiritual unity, his religion is the sphere where the deep self-contradiction of his existence becomes most intolerable. Granted that saving faith is the act of the whole man. But this can only mean that it is utterly beyond his power until God comes in His redeeming Word and makes him whole.

(2)

The God who comes in His Word is the living God. In His holiness and love He confronts the sinner in a personal encounter. Revelation is thus not a set of doctrines about God but God Himself in His gracious, mighty act of redemption. To believe in God means to respond to Him, to acknowledge His grace, to be reconciled to Him by receiving His forgiveness, to obey His will, and to live in His presence. Faith is the trust of a person in the personal God. This, then, is the first thing to be said in any exposition of saving faith—that it becomes possible only in the personal encounter of God with the sinner.

It is the prevailing fashion to interpret this divine-human encounter in terms of the *I-Thou* relationship. The contrast between the *I-Thou* and *I-Object* relationships is useful as a way of illustrating the chasm that divides saving faith in God from any merely notional knowledge or aesthetic contemplation of Him. But it will be a mistake to imagine that in these categories and in the existential philosophy from which they are borrowed we have at last found a metaphysical vindication of saving faith. The faith that justifies cannot itself be justified at the bar of any philosophy. We may not regard the divine-human encounter as an instance of *I-Thou* relationship in general, for it is a unique event. In spite of the analogy that holds between our trust in our fellow man and our trust in God, the differences here are more significant than the similarities. Our sensitiveness to the rights of personality in others belongs historically to our Christian heritage. Until we encounter God, the divine Thou, we never truly know and love our neighbour. And existential philosophy itself is more dependent than most philosophies upon the Christian Gospel. When, therefore, existential philosophers make faith the essence of man as man—utilizing those insights they have derived via Kierkegaard from the Gospel yet repudiating the source from which they spring—they are setting forth a view of man that is fundamentally false. Faith has once more become a *datum*, something in its own right, so to speak; a human power needing revelation, not in order that it may exist, but only in order that it may not be frustrated in its operation.

Certain views of faith are already disqualified, once we take in full seriousness the fact of revelation as God's *coming*. It is clearly impossible, for example, to identify faith with assent to a creed. If revelation is not an authoritative impartation of doctrines about God, but God actually present to us in a personal encounter, then a creed cannot be the object of our faith. We may go further: even if *per impossibile* we thought of God as revealing Himself by teaching us doctrines beyond our reason's power of discovery, even then faith would not be assent to the creed in which these doctrines were compendiously set forth. In the case supposed, we should assent to the doctrines only because we believed in the God who propounded them. We should believe them only because we *already* believed in Him and acknowledged His authority. This is not to say that assent to creeds plays no part in faith. But a creed—as the word itself implies—is the *expression* of our faith. It sets forth *what* we believe. Thus, while assent to a creed may be *an* act of faith—in the sense that it is an act of confession and witness—it can never be *the* act of faith, which is always our personal response to the God who personally encounters us.

Another inadequate view of faith may conveniently be dealt with here. There are those who go with us in recognizing that faith cannot be assent to a creed, and that revelation means not God teaching but God coming to us, who yet fail to do justice to the meaning of this divine coming. God comes to us in His incarnate Word, in Jesus Christ. Of course, all Christians are at one in affirming this. But the affirmation must be taken in its full meaning—God really comes to us in Jesus Christ, is present in Him, and present as the living, judging, and saving God. But it is not taken in its full meaning when faith is defined as believing "that God is like Jesus". Faith is this, but it is much more than this. And while it is true that God is like Jesus, this is far from being the whole, saving, truth of revelation. It may have a limited value as a stage on the way towards a more adequate conception of the Word of God, but only on condition that its provisional character is recognized. Taken as it stands, it is compatible with a merely humanitarian view of the Person of Christ. Jesus, that is to say, may be regarded as the supreme example of the self-revelation of God through human personality. What every good man reveals of the heart of God, Jesus reveals in fullest measure. But apart from its heretical leanings, this view of the revelation in Christ makes no real advance upon that which conceives the Word of God as a body of doctrine. Certainly we may more easily learn the divine lesson from a picture than from abstract statements, but here we are not concerned with learning lessons but with encountering the living God. In His revelation, God is always Subject—that is to say, He is always present as *God in Action*. In Jesus Christ, God does not send us a message or give us a portrait—He comes to us with a challenge, He encounters us. The gospels are not biographies of Jesus but records of the mighty acts of God in Him. The saving love of the Father in Christ is not displayed in a picture of how God feels towards us but in authoritative deeds. It was so for the men who encountered Jesus in the days of His flesh. For them, as for us, God was not showing something in the life and works of Jesus, but doing something—bringing in His Kingdom, destroying the works of the Devil, opening the gates of eternal life. These men did not say "God is like Jesus" but "God is acting in Jesus". Their faith bowed before the divine authority and they glorified in Him the mighty works of God. At the very centre of the revelation is a Victory won in the death and resurrection of Jesus. It is significant that the modern theologian who set most store by the self-portraiture of God in "the inner life of Jesus"—Wilhelm Herrmann—expressly excluded the Resurrection from the content of revelation. But the Resurrection cannot be excluded. The apostles and evangelists knew themselves to be commissioned to proclaim the Resurrection as the seal of that victory over sin, death, and the Devil that God had accomplished through His only-begotten Son. No; the Christian revelation is not static but dynamic. It is not a precious, antique portrait of a life once lived among men, to reverential contemplation of which we return when the world grows hard and tragic; it is not a serene word of assurance, echoing down the ages, to whose gracious accents we may listen when our spirits flag in their ceaseless fight against doubt and sin; or—rather—it is this only because it is more than this —the challenge of the living God who in Jesus Christ really comes, really encounters us.

(3)

When we say that God comes to us *in His Word*, does not this weaken our contention that in revelation God really *comes*? Does not a personal encounter between God and man demand that every intermediary shall be swept aside? What is this Word that, after all, must mediate between them? In every age of Christian history there have been those who have stumbled at this; for whom the apparent interposition of the Word between God and man has disqualified the Christian Gospel's claim to finality. Such have found, in some form of mysticism, a higher type of religion than Christianity, with its historical Jesus, its Bible, and its preaching Church. Now, while the term "The Word of God" may properly bear more than one meaning in Christian theology, we are using it in this essay in its primary and fontal sense. The Word of God to which our faith makes answer is the incarnate Word, Jesus Christ. When we speak of God's coming in His Word we are speaking of the revelation mediated to us by the Event of the Incarnation— by the life, death and resurrection of the Man whom our faith confesses as the Son of God. So far from making our encounter with the living God something less than personal, so that we can conceive a direct, mystical communion with Him more intimate than the dealings we have with Him in Christ, it is this Event of the Incarnation, and this alone, that assures us that God has really come, and that it is none other than God whose voice we hear and whose forgiveness we receive.

In the first place, the Word of God is no intermediary. Between God and man there may be many intermediaries, many media of revelation, but only one Mediator. Communication between men may be carried on by word of mouth or by writing. The articulated sounds and the written symbols are the media of the communication, but not the message itself; this is always a *meaning*, a "revelation" of mind and will made by a person to a person. So God uses human words, signs and acts as the instruments of His revelation, and human prophets and apostles as His messengers. But though the Word is given through these it is not in these. Even though God speaks His Word through the words and thoughts of prophets and apostles, these words and thoughts remain human words and thoughts, for ever distinct from the divine Word to which they bear testimony. The Word of God is His meaning, His gracious mind and purpose, His creative and redemptive Deed, His royal advent among men. This being the mediation, the Mediator is none other than God Himself in the person of His only-begotten Son. It is God who is in Christ *mediating*—reconciling the world unto Himself. When, therefore, the Christian creeds ascribe deity to Christ the Mediator, confessing Him as the only-begotten Son and incarnate Word of God "of one substance with the Father", they are making a grand affirmation about God—that in the Incarnation God Himself in very deed *comes* to us; that God Himself, God the Creator and Lord of our life, and no creature, whether an angel or a prophet, is the Mediator of His saving judgments and eternal love. The living God is the subject of which the Church's christology is the predicate. To confess the perfect humanity of Jesus is to confess that in Him God has really come to us, that the Incarnation is complete. The Word becomes flesh; and the God who reveals Himself in the Word remains the hidden God. It is because the unveiling of God in Christ is also a veiling that our encounter with Him is possible by faith alone. Many who were acquainted with Jesus of Nazareth saw in Him no more than a man. Some reverenced Him as prophet; others expected Him to lead a resistance movement against the

Romans; others, again, saw in Him a social reformer. Some scorned and hated Him as an enemy of the Law and a blasphemer, or despised Him as a gluttonous man and a winebibber. God has really come in the flesh; the veiling is complete. Only faith can penetrate the divine *incognito*, and see in the Galilean carpenter the promised Messiah and Saviour. And the sharp edge of the paradox of the Incarnation is not blunted with the passage of the centuries. To-day, the Christ who makes Himself our contemporary and meets us with His challenge and His promise is not recognized as our Saviour and Lord until the Spirit of God has opened our eyes.

But there is here more than the opening of the eyes; more than insight supernaturally vouchsafed to ordinary men. There is choice, decision. There is no personal encounter of God and man apart from freedom. Freedom first on God's side, who in His coming to us is and remains the God of grace, the God who is not only holy and loving but free. But because God is gracious—freely choosing us, freely coming to us, freely forgiving us—there is freedom on our side too. Certainly not that freedom that is ours here and now by virtue of our rational human nature; but a new freedom that God confers upon us in His gracious coming, to make it possible for us to believe in Him—freedom to answer His challenge and to acknowledge His grace; freedom to repent and to receive His forgiveness; freedom to be reconciled to Him and to our neighbour; freedom to live in hope of final redemption and eternal life.

The freedom of our faith is made possible only by the Word, the divine Mediator. An unmediated revelation would leave room for freedom neither in God nor in us. A god who manifested himself with the factualness of a lightning flash or an earthquake shock would establish no personal relation with us. He might operate on us but could not challenge us to decision. A god who showed himself to our minds as a self-evident truth or an inescapable deduction could compel our assent but could not win our allegiance. And if anybody were to object that, while God might have made Himself known to us in these compelling ways, it would still be open to us to choose whether we would obey and worship Him, we may reply that a god so revealed would not be worshipful. The god of the lightning flash would be known as Power but not as Grace; and a god of power without grace is either a demon or a mere natural force. As for the god of the self-evident truth he would be a mere Idea or algebraical expression. And here, perhaps, we may reply to those who seek a more intimate communion with God than is given to us in His incarnate Word. There is no nearer presence of God than His presence to us in Christ. The presence of God is His self-communication in a personal encounter with us. God may touch us without being observed and recognized. He may secretly inspire our thoughts and stimulate our feeling. He may be, He is, as inescapably present to us as the circum-ambient air. But until He speaks we do not know Him; until He imparts His meaning, sharing with us His mind and will, we cannot truly believe in Him. We cannot transcend the personal en-counter, the relationship. To think away the relationship is to think away not only faith with its freedom but God and His grace, and to be left with a Force that acts upon us as things.

But there is another reply we may make, equally pertinent to a discussion of the nature of faith. The suggestion that we might yet choose to obey and worship a god otherwise known than in a personal encounter betrays ignorance of the in-dissoluble unity of faith's knowledge and faith's obedience. The very knowledge of God that is ours in the personal en-counter of faith with the Word is itself a matter of choice. God not only will not compel us to obey Him; He will not compel us to know Him. He leaves us free to turn our backs upon Him. Though His Word is the Light of the world, we may yet choose to walk in darkness. The Light has come to us, yet we must come to the Light—and of our own free choice. To know God is to obey Him, and to obey Him is to know Him. For faith's knowledge of God is acknowledgment of Him who comes— acknowledgment of Him *as God*.

(4)

Paul says of the pagan Gentiles that "knowing God, they glorified Him not as God, neither gave thanks" (Romans 1: 21). What the Apostle contrasts here with the true knowledge of God is not sheer ignorance but error; and not intellectual error,

primarily, but a distorted perverse knowing, a misknowing of
God that is rooted in a decision against God, in man's refusal
to let God be God and Lord over him. Man is willing, anxious
even, to have God on his side. Man needs God's bounty and His
protection, and to secure these he is ready enough to offer a
quid pro quo in sacrifices and ritual observances. What man
is not ready to do is to accept God's lordship and to admit
His absolute sovereignty; and, while confessing his need of
God's pardon, man is more than reluctant to recognize that
God's pardon cannot be bought. He knows God, yet does not
know Him as God; for he does not and will not know His grace.
And, not knowing grace, he does not know himself as a sinner
whose sole hope in this life and the next is in God's free mercy.
To acknowledge God as God, as the holy and loving Creator
and Redeemer, upon whose unbought, unmerited loving-
kindness to us in Christ utterly depend our reconciliation to
Him and our redemption unto life everlasting—how is this
possible for us except as entailing an acknowledgment of our
guilt and helplessness, and the renunciation of our pride that
wills to know God and have Him only on terms that do not
shame us in our own eyes? If we will not know ourselves as
sinners, we cannot know God as gracious and merciful. Yet
only the Word that speaks of mercy can make us know the
depth of our need of mercy. This does not mean that we have
no hint of our sinfulness before the Word comes to us. As there
is, apart from the Word in Christ, a dim, distorted knowledge
of God, so also is there an uneasy consciousness of sin and
frustration, which finds expression in fear of God's wrath and
hostility towards Him. But what sin and guilt really mean we
never know except in the Word that gives us assurance that
our sin is "covered" and our guilt taken away. That is why, for
the believer, the Word of God brings the most precious of divine
gifts—reconciliation and forgiveness. But that is also why, for
the natural man, the Word is an affront and the offer of pardon
an intolerable offence.

To acknowledge God, therefore, is also to acknowledge
oneself as the sinner to whom His Word of forgiveness is
addressed. And to acknowledge oneself as a sinner is to renounce
that sinful self and to repent of sin. We cannot speak of faith

without speaking also of sin, faith's opposite. Faith is repentance and renunciation—a being crucified to our egoistic selves and to the world. But what is sin? And what does it mean to be crucified to the world? When Paul spoke of saving faith as a being conformed to Christ's death and resurrection, he meant what he said. His metaphors were not rhetorical hyperboles. We may be sure he did not say afterwards to himself or his friends: "Of course, when I wrote that the Christian must be crucified to the world, I was using a somewhat violent and exaggerated expression. What I really meant was that the Christian must fight down the impulses of his lower nature, and follow the promptings of his better self." No, he surely did not say this, or mean it. It is true that Paul reminds us, again and again, that we are committed to a warfare against the flesh. There are impulses to be resisted and a body to be buffeted and kept in subjection. But behind the daily acts of renunciation lies the great renunciation—faith. What the believer renounces is not only his lower nature but *himself*. For him, salvation is not the strengthening of his nobler against his baser part, but new life from the dead; not a purifying and refining of the personality, but a resurrection and a new creation. The acknowledgment that not his fleshly impulses alone but his entire spiritual existence lies under the judgment of God—this is his pride's crucifixion. His daily warfare against temptations calls him to acts of renunciation and repentance, because, even though justified, he is a sinner still. He has been reconciled, but not yet redeemed. His perfect sanctification and complete redemption lie beyond this present life, and are his here and now only by faith, by the assurance and hope that are given him in the promises of God, and which he hears and keeps alive in his heart through the power of the Holy Spirit.

What, then, is sin, which we have called the opposite of faith? We have said that it is our refusal to acknowledge God as God; it is our decision to turn our backs on the living God in order that we may worship an idol. Now we have to see that, entailed in this refusal to acknowledge the real God is our refusal to acknowledge our real selves. Here, too, we take our flight from reality and cherish a lie.

Our "lower nature" of fleshly passion may indeed be our

enemy, but this lower nature is not beyond redemption. By grace, it may be the servant of righteousness instead of a "procuress to the Lords of Hell". But this "better self"—what of him? Painfully and unremittingly we build him up, this self of our pride. He is the self we want to believe in, and want our fellows to believe in, too. He is respectable, moral, religious, even. He is never implicated in our regrettable lapses. For our sins—which, of course, we cannot deny—we blame our lower nature. We committed them, yet we were "not ourselves" when the temptations ambushed us. Not the unchastity, the violence, the deception, or the cruelty—not any of these *sins* or their like is our real sin. These are but fruits upon the tree of our wickedness; external symptoms of our deep-seated malady. Our *sin*, our heart of sinning, is that we identify ourselves with our "better self", trusting in him and hiding in him, instead of trusting and hiding in the infinite mercy of God.

When, in faith, we hear and respond to the Word of God, we can no longer evade our responsibility for our sins. We cannot hide behind our "better self", but are constrained to confess that we are sinners, and that God alone is our refuge. Our "better self" stands revealed as the creature of our wishful thinking—as a thing of pasteboard and tinsel with no life in him. Our faith renounces him, and repents of the proud, vain imaginings that attributed reality to the unreal, truth to a lie, and saving power to a bloodless shade. We renounce him, and ourselves who trusted in him. Because we are still sinful, even though justified and believing men, the ghost will continue to haunt us. But now, by grace, we know him for the impostor he is, and may contemplate with a smile his foolish posing. Yet the smile is a wry one and our amusement is grim. Left to ourselves, we are gullible still. Unless God continually comes to us in His Word and renews our faith by His Holy Spirit, not all our native shrewdness and sense of humour will be able to save us from again falling victims to self-deception and unreality.

(5)

We have insisted that faith is essentially *act*—the act of acknowledgment of God as God, the *decision* to surrender to

His grace and to renounce the egoistic sinful self. But an act presupposes a capacity, or power of acting. Even if we recognize that the natural man has no power to believe savingly in God, surely the Word of God in its coming creates such a power in the believer? Unless, after he has heard and responded to the Gospel, the believer possesses a new nature to which a capacity for faith or disposition to believe properly belongs, is it not meaningless to speak of regeneration and the *life of faith*? Overemphasis upon faith as an act seems to obscure, and even to deny, the continuity of Christian experience. As one critic puts it: "if faith lies only in acts of decision, it would seem to be like the telegraph posts without the wires."[1] There is certainly a difficulty here. But when we deny that there is, even in the believer, any permanent capacity for believing, we are not denying that his experience is psychologically continuous, or that it is different from what it would have been had he never heard and heeded the Gospel. The believer is not a case of dissociated personality, one half of which is entirely unaware of the experiences and acts of the other half. Though his faith is a miracle, the believer is a man and not a monstrosity. He does not pass from the act of faith into a limbo of unconsciousness where he is utterly unmindful of what has happened to him in the coming of the Word until a second advent of that Word re-creates for him the possibility of believing. Of course there is continuity here; there really is *a life* of faith. What, then, do we mean by saying that faith is essentially *act* and at the same time denying the existence, even in the regenerated man, of a power or capacity of believing?

An act of thinking presupposes a permanent capacity for thought. When we say "Smith knows Latin", we are attributing to him an abiding background of knowledge and experience that enables him to read Latin texts. Smith may spend no more than a small part of his conscious life in this pursuit. To say nothing of his hours of unconsciousness, Smith is not turning over his stores of classical scholarship when he is eating his dinner, or playing golf, or listening to a symphony. Yet, even when his thoughts are furthest from it, Smith knows Latin. For knowledge of Latin is one of his intellectual

[1] A. R. Whately, *The Focus of Belief*, p. 12

possessions, a piece of mental capital which he may use for his own cultural enrichment or allow to atrophy and be lost. But is not this also true of Smith's faith—assuming him to be a believer? Must not we credit him with a *capacity* for faith, even when he is so occupied with worldly things that for the moment he is not thinking about God at all?

There are two points to be made in reply to this. First, the suggested analogy between our acts of thinking and the act of faith does not hold. The believer is a man "in Christ"— and that Pauline phrase must be taken in all literal seriousness. The believer lives, not by his knowledge of God but by God's knowledge of him. His confession is not: "I know", but "I am known". The abiding background of faith, the continuity of the believer's life and experience, is not any capacity in himself but the unfailing love and mercy of God in Christ. We speak here of no mere psychological continuity but of a continuity in grace. The believer cannot summon up at will the faith that overcomes the world. If he must be saved by the purity and vigour of his faith, by its heroic venture and self-sacrifice, or by its constancy under trial, then he is of all men most miserable. His faith—so far as it is his, springing from the powers of his nature—is at best a faithless, failing thing. But when, through weariness, his prayer falters into silence, the Spirit makes intercession for him; and when he loses his hold on God, he is still upheld by the Everlasting Arms.

Then, too, although faith is truly an act, it is not one among other acts of our everyday experience, or at their level. It is a decision, but is not to be reckoned among other decisions. Even when we say that faith is "decision for Christ", we do not reach the heart of the matter. The ground of our faith is God's decision concerning us, declared and made effective in His Word. And the human analogue of this divine decision—our faith— is not the choosing of Christ above other lords, or the Kingdom of God above other causes, though such a choice, repeated again and again, is entailed by it and manifests it. When the Word of God is truly heard and acknowledged, our human existence stands revealed as being in itself decision. Not a series of isolated acts of decision, but life-as-decision—this is the essence of faith. Thus, the act of faith lies at the root of all Christian choices and judgments; it is the obedience to God's Word that draws in its train all our day-to-day acts of ethical obedience. For faith *is* obedience. We do not *first* know God and *then* decide to give Him our service and praise. Because faith's knowledge of God is acknowledgment of Him as God, it is and must be itself obedience—the act of surrender in which our whole existence is utterly committed. To detach faith's knowledge from faith's obedience is to lose the true meaning of both. Apart from faith's obedience, faith's knowledge shrinks into a theoretical knowledge of God from which our duty regarding Him would have to be deduced. Such a theoretical knowledge—in itself questionable—is emphatically not the knowledge given to us in the divine-human encounter, in which we find we cannot know God in His holy love and mercy without casting ourselves at His feet and surrendering to His gracious will. And obedience, detached from faith's knowledge of God, is no longer true obedience but a "works-righteousness", complacent or despairing. We cannot obey the Law until we hear and obey the Gospel. Faith is this hidden obedience to the Gospel, manifesting itself in overt acts—choices, attitudes, deeds. And faith remains hidden even in its manifestation. For these overt acts are not materially different from those of the non-believer. Only God knows whether they are truly good; whether their hidden spring is the gratitude and obedience of faith or the pharisaic egoism and faithless anxiety of sin.

And so we end with the *hiddenness* of faith. Even here we trace the pattern of the Incarnation. The believer is no "religious genius" but an ordinary man whose faith, miracle though it be, need make no great stir in a world avid of the sensational and the bizarre. He does not claim as his own the faith by which he lives; it is the gift of God in His continual coming. Christ is his hope and the Holy Spirit his strength and his consolation. And with his life's treasure in his Father's keeping he waits in penitence, obedience, and trust for the Day of Redemption when he shall see God face to face in the eternal Kingdom.

V

THE CHURCH CATHOLIC AND REFORMED
The Missing Half of the Church's Life To-day

By D. T. JENKINS, M.A., B.D.

Jesus Christ is the Lord and Saviour of the congregation as a congregation. It is the congregation, as the congregation, which has to justify its activity to Him. The ecclesiastical order has its life solely in the congregation, but the congregation has not its life solely in the ecclesiastical order.[1]

ALL Protestants would agree with that statement of Karl Barth's, in theory, but many would have to confess that their churches deny it, in practice. We insist on the reality of the priesthood of all believers; we assert that the Word of God in Scriptures must be accessible to all the people; we give to the congregation certain formal rights; but the congregation itself as a unit in the life of the Church very often hardly exists. Even on the theological level, and even among those churches where the congregation has a good deal of life and reality, very little work is done upon the nature and structure of the congregation. The Reformed Revival has made us see with fresh vividness the importance of the Word and Sacraments in the life of the Church, but it has not as yet paid anything like the same attention to the congregation to which they are addressed and to the nature of that "discipline and crisis" which they engender in it when they are faithfully administered.

Barth's words quoted above are obviously directed against Roman Catholicism, and Roman Catholicism to-day, when it is rediscovering what it calls the apostolate of the laity, has to justify to itself the fact that as it has developed in history the congregation has its life solely in the ecclesiastical order. Roman Catholicism insists that the bishop possesses the fullness

[1] *The Knowledge of God and the Service of God*, Hodder and Stoughton, 1938, p. 186

of church order in his own person, and any hierarchical status which any other member of the church possesses must be conferred upon him by the bishop. The congregation has no such gift or status conferred upon it as a body. Indeed, in the structure of Roman Catholicism the congregation does not merely possess no rights, it does not exist as a unit of the Church's life. It possesses no recognizable identity apart from that of the individual members who make it up. Roman Catholicism speaks much of the Church as "the Body of Christ", but, for all practical purposes, it is the ministry which makes up the Body, while the congregation is "in ward" to the ministry.

The result of this is that the whole balance of the Church's life is destroyed. It is not always clearly seen that the imposing structure of Catholic church order is built up to conceal a gaping hole at the centre of the Church's life. Since the congregation as a unit does not exist, no spiritual authority can be given to it, and no responsible decisions entrusted to it. All responsible decisions must, therefore, come from above; and thus the natural tendency is to suppose that the further up you go the more authoritative the voice becomes. The ordering of the Church becomes similar to that of the British Civil Service, and it is not fanciful to see an analogy between the authoritarian structure of Roman Catholicism and the "passed to you, please" principle of Civil Service administration. The only man who is compelled by the system to take a really important spiritual decision is the man at the top, and the rest of the hierarchy, in greater or lesser degree, proceed on the basis of instruction or precedents. The result is that the discipline and crisis engendered by a personal Word, speaking to the condition of the individual man of faith in the context of the common life of the Body, is lost; and, in its place, is put, at best, the struggle to conform to a static pattern of ideal holiness, and, at worst, perfunctory acts of minimum obligation in obedience to the demands of the clergy. Preaching and Sacraments do not speak the living Word of a personal God engaged in personal dealings with His people, giving them guidance for another stage in their pilgrimage to the Promised Land. Divine service is not, as it should be, a continuation of

173

the Sacred History. It is the performance of an ordered pattern of ritual on the part of the ministry in which the congregation have no form of effective participation and in which there is no place for anything new in the life of the Church to emerge. Certain tendencies, even in Roman Catholicism, as we shall see, resist this, and it is nothing like so true of some forms of Anglo-Catholicism and of Orthodoxy; but that this is the dominant note of Catholicism, as such, it is surely impossible to deny.[1]

It is the supreme merit of Protestantism that it does start by clearly grasping the fact that the "ecclesiastical order must have its life in the congregation". In Protestantism, it is the free Christian man, who has found again his true humanity in fellowship with his brethren, around whom the Church's life revolves, and not the Pope or the bishop. This fact constitutes one of the chief justifications of Protestantism as against Catholicism; and even empirical modern Protestantism, with all its many failings, has never allowed it completely to disappear from its life. At the same time, it cannot be asserted that even Protestantism at its best has ever very adequately understood or established the right relation between the congregation and the ecclesiastical order, or has paid enough attention to the building up of the congregation as an essential organ of the Church's life.

The different forms of Protestantism have, of course, varied considerably in the place they have given to the congregation. Both Lutheranism and Presbyterianism have strongly emphasized the priesthood of all believers, and the latter has given a great place to the vocation of the individual believer in the secular world; but both have set serious limits on the sphere of the congregation's responsibility, and, in both, the congregation has in practice frequently been allowed to

[1] cf. here the illuminating comment of M. Jarret-Kerr, C.R., on recent Roman Catholic novels, in *The Student Movement*, March–April, 1946, p. 98. "Where the religious background is most convincing and best integrated into the theme, it is entirely *futureless*: the stress is upon the deep survivals, the grip upon the instincts, the strength and weaknesses of the collective unconscious. This must be so to some extent of all great literature: but there the traditions, the instinctive roots, are appealed to not as something past, but as something from the past, living in the present, and still to be reckoned with in the future; here, in R.C. fiction, the past seems to survive into the present not as a real part of it, and the future must be bent back to meet it"

degenerate into the position of an audience for sermons. Methodism has certainly emphasized, as few other churches have, the importance of using the spiritual gifts imparted to the laity; but its church organization is both highly clerical- ized and built up on the basis of evangelistic expediency, rather than of clear theological principle. The ordinary church member has many opportunities of realizing his Christian vocation in Methodism, but the congregation, as such, has little corporate existence or sense of being an essential organ of the Church's life. Congregational churches, together with some of the Baptist churches, can claim to have taken the congregation as part of the essential structure of the Church's life more seriously than any other part of the Church. They have endeavoured to establish the Church Meeting as a means through which the whole membership of the Church in a particular place can strive to realize their common vocation as the people of God, and strive to bring themselves into the obedience of the Word of God which is declared to them in sermon and sacrament. That this is a contribution of the first importance to the whole Church's understanding of Church Order is undeniable; but it has to be qualified by the admission that Congregationalism has not always seen sufficiently clearly the link between the life of the Church Meeting and the regular ministration of the Word and Sacraments, nor has it ever worked out a satisfactory relationship between the life of the local Church and of the great Church.[1]

It is always very difficult to generalize about the position of the Church of England on any matter, but it is peculiarly so in this instance. The congregation has always had some rights in the Church of England but, at the same time, it has always been difficult to distinguish it from the community in general. In more recent times, however, determined efforts, both official and unofficial, have been made to give the congregation a more vital place in the life of the Church of England. It may be that the Church of England will succeed better than many

[1] It is unfair, however, to say that Congregationalism has no sense of the great Church and no belief in a cosmic redemption. Continental theologians often examine Congregationalism as an idea which can be conveniently criticized in text-books, rather than as a form of existing church polity which has been given a reasoned theological justification by Reformed theologians with a "high" doctrine of the Church

other more definitely Protestant churches in restoring the
missing half of the Church's life in our own day.

It is my view that the best hope of the revival of a truly
oecumenical theology, and of the restoration of a common
Church order, to churches at present divided lies in the attempt
to re-establish the congregation as an effective part of the
structure of Church Order. There are several promising signs
which point in this direction. The experience of those churches
which have confessed their faith in the midst of persecution,
whether in the occupied lands of Europe and in Germany or in
the Far East, has been that the congregation has come alive as
a real organ of spiritual fellowship and responsibility when
pressure from the enemies of the Church has forced upon every
member a clear decision for or against Christ. In England, the
Free Churches are showing an increasing concern that their
Church Meetings should again be what they were originally
intended to be; and, in the Church of England, the movement
to build up a parish meeting around the parish eucharist,
where members of the congregation meet together to discuss
the implementation of their common responsibility for living
together as the church in the setting of their parish, is con-
stantly growing in power and influence. Whether the Liturgical
Movement in Roman Catholicism, which has an aim in many
ways similar, is strong enough to resist other strains in Roman
Catholicism with which it is incompatible remains to be seen;
but especially when it is related to the Christian personalism
and the defence of democracy of many Catholic philosophers
and theologians, it certainly constitutes a hopeful sign. Above
all, the widespread attempts of churches in many lands to
express their Christian vocation more effectively, in terms of
the life of the society in which they are set, represent what may
turn out to be the most powerful means of all of building up
again the missing half of the Church's life. Even though in their
beginnings these movements are often highly centralized, and
appear to have little direct relation to the life of ordinary
congregations in ordinary neighbourhoods, they must, in the
end, make a substantial difference to ordinary congregations
by making the whole Christian community see its vocation
in a different light. When the Church is genuinely concerned

that its obedience become a total obedience, in industry and politics and education, as well as in personal relations, and uses specifically theological criteria and not those of current idealism or progressivism for its action in these spheres, then the immediate service of the sanctuary ceases to be the only recognizable form of Church Service; and the layman ceases to be, as otherwise he inevitably does in practice become, a Christian of more or less inferior order to the clergy. As this movement develops, and it is being taken up in Catholic and Reformed churches alike, it should give all churches a new perspective in which to see differences of order and ministry, and may very well create a healthier atmosphere for their discussion.

If a new unity is to be achieved, however, through our recovery of the missing half of the Church's life, two tasks lie before us. First, we must see how the whole apparatus of Church order, ministry, preaching, sacrament, church meeting, loses its purpose if the "discipline and crisis" of the Word of God in which the Church must live if she is to be obedient is not engendered. Church order, as Barth has so decisively shown in his Gifford Lectures, is not an end in itself but is the servant of the Church's service of God over the whole range of her life on earth. Secondly, we must consider again what is involved for the corporate life of the congregation in the fulfilment of this obedience. "The godly discipline" must be reinstated, in a way less open to the dangers of legalism and triviality than in traditional Protestantism, and with special reference to the corporate life of the congregation in the world of to-day. We can thank God that the Word and the Sacraments are again receiving something of their proper place in Protestantism, and that we have seen with new force how their faithful administration are necessary marks of the Church's presence. But, if we mean what we say about them, we must go on to ask with the same theological integrity and seriousness what should happen in a church where the Word is truly preached and the Sacraments faithfully administered according to God's ordinance. We must now ask, in the most concrete terms, what difference the revival of Reformed theology makes, not only to our preaching, but also to our Christian walk and conversation in the world. That, once stated, is obvious; but yet it is a task which we have sometimes shown signs of neglecting in favour of ever more eloquent and scholarly statements of generalized Christian doctrine. In particular, we must consider the distinctive nature of our corporate obedience as "the congregation which includes the ecclesiastical order" in a new light. We need a restatement of the nature and duties of the Church Meeting which will safeguard it from the errors of secular democracy and the dangers of unbalanced individualism which so easily beset it. The Church Meeting must be set within the framework of a comprehensive Church order, covering the whole range of Catholic Church order, interpreted in terms of the dynamic Reformed understanding of the sovereignty of the Word of God in His Church. This may sound impossible of achievement, but it is, in point of fact, in this direction that a good deal of the most serious and practical oecumenical discussion is moving. What is certain is that unless our churches possess all these elements in their life they will not possess the fullness of their catholicity. For, without them, they will still be existing merely on the level of ideas or of hollow outward forms, and not genuinely embodying the Christian Way as a life lived together by the family of God on this earth.

In the fulfilment of this task, the work of Barth is of the greatest significance. He has not striven merely to give new weapons of self-justification to existing Protestantism, but, as Dr. F. W. Camfield has said,[1] he is a great oecumenical theologian, who is hammering out a *theologia viatoris* in whose light all who are in covenant together to live by the power of Jesus Christ can walk. He is the only theologian of our generation who is producing a theology of oecumenical range and sweep; and he does this by using the proper method of oecumenical theology, bringing all his findings remorselessly to the bar of Scripture, and showing the greatest sympathetic sensitivity to what doctors of the Church in all ages and communions have testified concerning God and His ways with His people. There are, however, four specific ways in which Barth's teaching

[1] In an article on "Barth on Predestination", *Theology*, Vol. XLVI, No. 271, p. 8

helps up towards a right understanding of the place of the congregation in the life of the Church.

First, he has shown us with new insight and clarity that Christ and He alone must rule in His Church, and that because of the infinite subtlety of human sin our effort to ensure that He does must be much more all-embracing and complicated than we have often realized. The Church cannot serve Christ merely by taking itself for granted and assuming that all is well with it because it goes through a regular routine of services and maintains a reasonable level of unimaginatively decent conduct. Nor can it do so by hurrying busily in the wake of the *zeitgeist* and trying to conform itself to what men believe to be the most enlightened and progressive ideas of their own time. Nor yet can it take refuge behind the belief that it is securely buttressed by an unchallengable apostolic authority handed down in unbroken historical succession or by an infallible power which can always be relied upon in an emergency. The Church can only be sure that Christ reigns in her midst when she stands before the searchlight of the Word of God as the Scriptures declare it and as it is addressed to her own particular situation, and there tries as a Church to obey it. It is always a task which confronts the Church, a constant challenge to win a victory over its own unbelief and sin. Christ never gives Himself over into the charge of the Church, so that she can rest content in Him as her secure possession. He is the Master and she the servant, and He has provided Church order as the means by which she tries to ensure that her service is faithful service. Barth has, therefore, forced upon us the question not merely whether our preaching and sacraments constitute faithful witness to Jesus Christ but also whether the congregation is taking heed of them and trying to live by His power. This, in turn, has delivered theology from false academicism by making clear that it must always be the servant of a preaching which is addressed to the actual existing body of Christ as it serves and fails to serve Him in this world. Likewise, by linking together the Church's theological task and the life of the congregation, Barth has helped us to see how taking the congregation seriously again as an effective unit in the Church's life does not necessarily mean the surrender of the Church to "lay religion", the superficial impressionism of the amateur in religious matters.

The second special service Barth has rendered to us in our understanding of the place of the congregation in the life of the Church has been through his powerful re-affirmation of the truth of the Reformers' doctrine of justification by faith. Faith, to Barth, as to Brunner, is "the totality-act of the whole personality", the act whereby we appropriate for ourselves the gift of true manhood offered to us in the humanity of Jesus Christ and thus recover the freedom of the Sons of God which we had lost through sin. This is important for our understanding of the congregation because it decisively reasserts the vocation of each believer to take a responsible part in the life of the Body of Christ, a vocation he denies only by denying that he has found again his true manhood and freedom in Christ. Yet, justification by faith is no doctrine of "Protestant individualism". Because it means the recovery of our true manhood in Christ, it means also the recovery of a right relation to our neighbour as we find him alongside ourselves in Christ. It means that we are "no more strangers and sojourners but fellow-citizens with the saints and of the household of God". Thus, the man who understands what is involved in justification by faith cannot be content with a churchmanship which consists merely in private devotion or in obedience to the dictates of the clergy. He needs to enter a living community of Christian people who are trying together, each according to his several vocation, to testify to the reality of that "Jerusalem which is at unity within herself".

All this, of course, is no more than one of the central messages of the Reformation, and it has been proclaimed in the churches of the Reformation ever since Martin Luther wrote his Primary Works. But it has been Barth and some of his colleagues who have made us see again the profundity and range of this doctrine and how radically it contradicts the self-centredness of modern man. That self-centredness has entered into our very way of looking at the world, so that even our theology was infected with it and we became more concerned with examining our own religious experience than with standing in the presence of God; and it has been a great achievement of prophetic and critical theology on their part to show us again how a leap of justifying faith in Jesus Christ must be made, if we are to break through the prison-house of self-centredness into the real world where we find God and ourselves and our neighbour.

Thirdly, Barth has made us see again that Church order is a divine ordinance which is designed to maintain men together in the Christian life in terms of their existence in this sinful world in which we are set. Church order is not mere organization, the formal element which must be present to keep the institution going when the "spiritual" element is absent or burning very low: nor is it a structure possessing self-generating power of its own, which can keep going without having faithful people to work it. It is a rough shape which Christ's Body has, in this world, adapted to the kind of world in which it is found, a shape whose outlines may not always be clear to the external observer but whose content is always clear enough. Thus, the sermon is not meant to be an essay in providing spiritual thrills for an interested audience, but the Church's disciplined and concentrated attempt to listen to what God is saying to it out of the Scriptures for its guidance through this world. The Lord's Supper is not a memorial service to an absent Master but a means whereby He Himself is present in the midst, to guide and to sustain. Both sermon and sacrament are not channels whereby an impersonal grace is diffused to build up individuals unconsciously into the likeness of Christ. They are forms of encounter between Christ and His people where we know Him even as we are known on the acutest and most precise level of personal awareness. In the same way, the Scriptures are not a body of abstract propositions of faith nor a mine of proof-texts, but the record of the mighty acts of the living God in history; and when they are expounded in the context of our present experience they become an active force in our midst once more, and impel us to be the means whereby the Sacred History which they record is carried one step further according to the purpose of God.

The corollary of this dynamic understanding of Church order must be that the congregation cannot exist as so much neutral stuff to be impregnated with a grace automatically administered by the priesthood, nor as the detached spectators of the performances of eloquent preachers. It must be a living Body, always conscious of its corporate responsibility to its Head, and always needing, and looking for, and being impatient if it does not obtain, these acts of ministry which it must receive if it is to know the will of Christ and have power to obey it.

Fourthly, Barth's ruthless insistence that the lordship of Jesus Christ over the whole of life must be taken seriously, and his obstinate refusal as a theologian to be interested in any attempts to reach a *modus vivendi* between faith and unbelief through certain forms of natural law doctrine, provide a most powerful impulse towards Christian action in secular society. This is a side of Barth's work which is not clearly appreciated in this country, where the impression that his teaching is a form of Pietist Evangelicalism still persists in the face of all the evidence. It is not an accident that those churches on the continent which have felt most strongly the impact of Barth's teaching, such as those of France, Holland and Switzerland, have been foremost in seeking to reclaim for Christian allegiance areas of life which had previously been given up for lost. Barth's emphasis on Christ's sole lordship does not mean that we are to retreat into a private religious world of our own. On the contrary, it insists that there is no longer a private religious world; for Jesus Christ has risen from the dead and all things must be brought under His dominion, whether thrones or principalities or powers. Christians cannot rest content as long as His lordship is denied in any nook or cranny of the universe, however secular or technical or religiously-neutral it may declare itself to be. "The existence of the Church in the world, the fact that she must venture to speak the Word of God to it, means a *sanctification* of the world, preliminary but none the less real."[1] Barth's uncompromising reassertion of the sovereignty over the whole world of the Triune God whose name is known only in Jesus Christ may yet do more to re-establish the Christian civilization of Europe than all our well-meaning attempts to find a platform upon which "all men of goodwill" can unite without prejudice of principle in the defence of "spiritual values".

It is clear that this insistence on the lordship of Christ

[1] *The Knowledge of God and the Service of God*, p. 219

over the whole of life, and the impulse to seek to obey Him in every sphere of life which arises out of it, is of great importance for our attempts to recreate the congregation as an effective and responsible organ of the Church's life. It is true that many of our attempts to obey Christ in secular society will not and cannot be done by the congregation itself as a whole, but by individuals and groups who have particular vocations to work in various specific areas of life. But this activity streaming out from the worshipping community is one of the chief parts of that half of the Church's life which is missing, and when large numbers of members of the Church are taking part in it the congregation itself is bound to become more alive and more conscious of itself as a working fellowship. As its members are forced to take real Christian decisions in the real world, they will come to look for it much more for guidance and inspiration and support. Further, the congregation itself, as well as the individual members who compose it, has responsibilities to the world in general, and it is only when it genuinely believes that this whole universe is one which Christ has reclaimed for Himself that it will achieve the measure of authority, confidence, discipline and humility to enable it to undertake them.

To restore the missing half of the Church's life is the chief special task of Christians in this generation, when we have been driven to see how far our civilization has departed from its Christian origins and how unconsciously secularized much of our own life as Christians had become. There is much that we must know for the fulfilment of this task which Karl Barth cannot tell us; much that we can learn only from the attempt to perform the task itself. But it is only if we take heed to what he has made us see again of God and His ways with His Church that we can begin to hope to succeed.

VI

THE CRISIS IN PHILOSOPHY

By H. A. Hodges, M.A. D.Phil.

THE story of modern philosophy is a story of crisis. A branch of human activity which has played a great part in man's life since the early days of ancient Greece is now involved in perplexities which cast doubt upon its future. A branch of thought to which Christians have been not unwilling to appeal in support of their fundamental beliefs is now more and more seriously examining its own credentials. Why is this, and what does it mean for the Christian?

Philosophy is not one of those activities, like tool-making and artistic expression, which seem to be coeval with man. What we know as philosophy began, in the great culture-centres, in the course of the first millennium before Christ. It was part of the great intellectual revolution by which the millennium is characterized, the revolution which gave us mathematical science and the beginnings of physics, social and political theory, and the first idea of a planned society, and drastic reform and criticism in the sphere of religion. Philosophy grew up in the midst of all this and was indeed its presiding spirit. The critical and creative mind of man became self-conscious, and brought its own proceedings under examination. The methods and principles of thought in its various employments were analysed, and the relations between science, morals and politics, and religion, were set forth in a reasoned scheme. What men sought from philosophy was nothing less than the principle of unity by which their diverse concerns might be held together, and the failure to achieve a philosophical synthesis would have meant for them the disintegration of their culture.

It is therefore no wonder that philosophy in the first few centuries of its existence attained a degree of perfection and a height of prestige which have remained archetypal for it ever since. The tradition of philosophical thought still flows from what was achieved in the first three hundred years, and until very recent times there was little else in philosophy but the attempt to dot the i's and cross the t's of Plato and Aristotle. Not until the seventeenth and especially the eighteenth century do we find the beginning of a new movement, which, increasingly predominant as time goes on, calls all past achievements in question and boldly asks how philosophy can survive.

The change is due, of course, to the new atmosphere brought into all intellectual questions by the steady advance of modern science, and to some extent the situation can truly be depicted as a challenge to philosophy by science itself, which comes forward as a rival means of integration. But when we look deeper we see that the challenge arises also from within philosophy itself, and the whole modern development in philosophy is nothing else but the elaboration of this challenge. What distinguishes modern philosophy from that of earlier ages is, above all, the seriousness with which the question of first principles and presuppositions is now taken. It was always clear that there are certain first principles and presuppositions without which the work of thought would be impossible. The ancients and the medievals knew that. But they supposed that there was no doubt what these principles and presuppositions were, and since there was only one set of them in possession of the intellectual field, it was easy to slip into regarding them as self-evident. A great structure of ideas, embracing not only philosophy but also the physical sciences, was built up on certain principles which were themselves little more than a codification of common sense, and the serene confidence of the *philosophia perennis* in these its principles was never shaken until in modern times a revolution was wrought in the physical sciences. But the new movement which begins about the time of Galileo is based upon a hitherto unknown method and a set of principles which differed from those previously adopted, and even in some points contradicted them. This is the Danaan gift which modern science brings to philosophy: a conflict of principles. Hence the crisis of philosophy in our time.

There is no need to tell the story in detail. The main lines of it are well known. By the time of Kant it had been made pretty clear that first principles and absolute presuppositions are neither self-evident truths nor empirical generalizations, and that the only justification we can give of them is a purely pragmatic one: that they enable thought to go ahead. It was seen that, in knowing, the human mind is much more active than we used to think; that knowledge includes more construction and less direct insight; and that the lines on which our constructions are made correspond more to the functional necessities of a discursive mind, and less to the inherent nature of the known object, than had been supposed. It follows, of course, that our thought-processes are not to be trusted further than we can check them, and that when it is a question of realities beyond the range of observation and experiment, no knowledge of them is possible at all. This daunting conclusion is supported by the history of philosophy, seen, as Kant saw it, as a tale of perpetually recurring antinomies. And even this was only a beginning. As the nineteenth century wore on, it became evident that categories and first principles have a history which is to some considerable extent governed by factors other than purely cognitive ones, and that types of philosophy can be correlated with psychological types with a disconcerting regularity. In short, the modern movement in philosophy is in great part a movement towards a radical subjectivism and relativism.

What does all this mean for a Christian? That depends on the relation between philosophy and Christianity. But this relation itself has a history, and here, too, old habits of thought are being called in question.

The relation between philosophy and Christianity will always be a live issue both for philosophers and for Christians, because the two are working to some extent in the same field. This was obvious from the very moment that the two came into contact at all. The Greeks, by virtue of their philosophy, were the first people in Europe to see and state clearly the abiding problems of human life. A nation with rich creative powers, yet also capable of radical self-criticism, attempting great cultural tasks with limited material and human resources, they early understood that man is finite and can build lastingly only by adopting a limited aim; and they understood that, even so, his achievement is liable to be destroyed at any time by the incalculable forces of nature from without, or by his own unbridled passions from within. Hence arose for them the great problems on which metaphysics and ethics are built. What is man's real nature and his place in the world process? How can he truly see his place, and if he gets this knowledge, how can he make it effective in his conduct? To ask these questions is to be led at once to the religious problem.

That the Greeks were so led is manifest in the fact that they, first of all Europeans, developed a critical and systematic theology. They were led, in fact, to decompose the primitive idea of a god into its constituent parts, and to recompound it on a critical basis. The primitive idea of a god is a logical hybrid, in which personal and impersonal elements are held together without any clear notion as to the relations between them. There is a personal name, a tradition of addressability, perhaps a myth in which the god behaves as a person among persons. Yet behind this façade the solid fact is, and is always felt to be, some process of nature or human nature, the round of the seasons or the erotic instinct. It is not a deliberate person-ification, but an uncritical muddle. But the Greeks cut the god-concept in two, setting on one side gods who are wholly personal, and wholly or mainly wise and good, and on the other side the laws of nature and the inscrutable power of fate. Which of these is supreme? Are the gods merely incidents in an im-personal world process? Or is the regular order of the *kosmos* the work of a supreme intelligence? If the latter, does He take note of individual men and their concerns? The highest flights of Platonic and Aristotelean speculation bring us at last to these plain religious issues, which the mighty figure of Socrates, with his belief in particular providences, living in the same age as Democritus, the prophet of impersonal law, had made inescapable.

To Jews and Christians, God's absolute kingship and His care for all His creatures are known more clearly and con-vincingly than to any Greek. Yet there was good reason why Jews and Christians should welcome the efforts made by Greek philosophy. Going out into a world of crude nature-worship and equivocal mythologies, preaching the unity of God and the sovereignty of moral purpose in the world, they found this voice already in the *agora*, speaking on very similar lines. It is written that God has not left Himself without a witness among any nation. Here then obviously is the witness as it came to the Greeks. So we are not surprised when St. Paul allows himself at moments to preach and argue like a Stoic, or even when Justin says that all who have ever lived by reason have been Christians whether they knew it or not, since there is no reason but the *Logos* who is Christ.

This indeed was an oversimplification; and some centuries passed before Christians, as a body, made up their minds about pagan learning in general or about philosophy in particular. Nor has there ever been a unanimous Christian view on the point. But there came into existence a type of theologian who found philosophy an aid to clear thinking about the Faith. St. Augustine found it in his own experience not merely an aid, but a propaedeutic; and, in his thinking and writing, philosophy and theology are so intermingled that it is hardly possible to separate them, for he philosophizes as a Christian, and understands the Faith as a philosopher. This alliance and mutual interpenetration became the normal relation between philosophy and theology from his time until the Reformation. Philosophy was taken to include a rational knowledge of the being and principal attributes of God; of man's nature and the natural law which embodies his duties to other men and to God; of the immortality of the soul, and the certainty of rewards and punishments after death. The value of such rational knowledge to the Christian is obvious. It clarifies and strengthens his hold on the truths of the Faith, and elevates belief into understanding. Whether a non-Christian could attain this knowledge was a more difficult question. It was easy to show that, as a matter of historical fact, no non-Christian philosopher ever had arrived at a doctrine of God and the soul which did not incorporate grievous errors; yet these non-Christian writers had not only built up an impressive structure of ideas about the natural world, but even in theology they had forged the tools with which the Christian could correct their mistakes. If it were not so, how could the Christian missionary find common ground on which to speak to those who, *ex hypothesi*, have not the light of faith to live by, but only that of reason? So, in the work of the great Dominican, St. Thomas, the claims of philosophy are generously endorsed by theology, and a sphere of natural reason is marked out where conclusions are reached which revealed theology may amplify, but cannot revise. And even in its own sphere, revealed theology talks a language learned from pagan philosophy, and defines the mysteries of the Faith in their categories. Nor is it only abstract thought which is affected, but also the devotional life; for the Catholic, ascetic discipline takes its categories, its techniques, and in a measure even its aims, from Greek philosophical sources, as well as from the Bible and Christian tradition.

The Reformation came, and this great synthesis was called in question and repudiated. The Reformation appeal to the Bible as the sole source of a true knowledge of God was not merely a preference for Hebraism over Hellenism, as for one culture over another. It was an appeal against all culture, as a man-made thing, to the Word of God before which all culture stands arraigned. Not that cultural activities are to be despised. Luther, who is most outspoken in his denunciations of "reason" or philosophy when regarded as an independent way to the knowledge of God, also recognized its value when used by one who has already drawn that knowledge from the proper source. In the wisdom of God, the world by its wisdom knew not God; but where saving faith has gone before, reason, like everything else in man, is transformed and rehabilitated by the power of the Resurrection. What reason cannot do is to bring us to saving faith in the first place; and until we have been brought to this faith (not merely an intellectual adherence to true propositions about God, but a total adherence to Him as Redeemer), reason is helpless even in its own sphere. As works done before justification, or before the grace of Christ and the inspiration of His Spirit, have the nature of sin, so also thinking done before justification and grace has the nature of error, and can itself be an obstacle to grace. Hence the words of Peter Boehler which so puzzled John Wesley before his Aldersgate experience: *mi frater, mi frater, excoquenda est ista tua philosophia.* Such was always the voice of the Reformation. It threw the church back upon the Word and its power, and challenged it to evaluate philosophy afresh and differently.

It was at the very moment when the Reformation issued its challenge that philosophy itself began to feel the impact of the new scientific ideas, and the process began which has driven modern philosophy so far along new paths. These paths lead far away from Christianity. In the gradual disintegration of the *philosophia perennis* during the last three centuries, the first parts of it to go were just those which had offered a basis for a positive understanding with Christianity, and as the process has gone further, it has ended by making modern philosophy a positively anti-Christian force.

In the first place, the position of God in philosophical thinking has radically changed. Before the eighteenth century, all European thinking (apart from individual eccentrics like Bruno or Spinoza) moved in a kind of two-dimensional framework. There was the horizontal line, on which man and nature stood side by side, and the vertical line which led up from them both to their source in God. The first effect of the new standard of evidence set up by scientific enquiry, and of the logical and epistemological critique to which this gave rise within philosophy, was to cast doubt on the vertical line. The horizontal plane is that of empirical knowledge; the world about us is a matter of observation. But the vertical line is a line of speculation, going up hazardously into a realm where theories cannot be checked. Such speculation first appears illegitimate, and then loses its appeal and becomes uninteresting, so that in the end the question ceases even to be asked. The horizontal line is left as the sole dimension of thought; and we do not feel any great constraint or narrowing of our range of thought by reason of this, because as we think less about God we think more and more about the relations between man and the world around him. This is the great issue which dominates philosophy in the nineteenth century, and the philosophical doctrines of the period can be classified according to the line they take about this issue. There is the naturalistic doctrine, which accepts in essentials the account of the world given by physical science, and treats man as a particular phenomenon arising within that system. There is the pantheist or panpsychist doctrine, which declares the world to be in some sense a living whole, and so not alien to man's higher aspirations.

And there are the various forms of idealism, which make man's consciousness the *locus* of the realization of the absolute idea or the absolute will. These doctrines fight for the pre-eminence, and their struggle is a great part of the history of philosophy in the nineteenth century. But they are all non-Christian and anti-Christian doctrines, and their conflicts with one another are shadow-conflicts in comparison with their common opposition to the Christian doctrine of God.

Secondly, the pantheist and idealist systems have an inherent tendency to sink the human individual in the "higher" unity of the Great Mind; and this tendency is powerfully reinforced by the recognition of all the ways in which our character, thought, and will are conditioned, nay, produced and moulded into shape, by historical and social factors. The exploration of all this is part of the advance in social science which constitutes one of the notable achievements of the last 150 years, but it has made an impact on philosophy which is not altogether to be welcomed. Hegel's speculative formula, that the community or state is the true moral substance of which the individual is a mode, expresses the sense of this movement, by which the human person is reduced to a casual confluence of impersonal forces and mass trends. The consequences of this are serious not only for Christianity but also for ordinary morality; for, on the one hand, the idea of objective moral principles, as embodied in the traditional doctrine of natural law, is undermined by the realization of the extent to which standards are historically relative; and, on the other hand, individual responsibility is undermined also by the suggestion that the mass trends are the only reality.

Immanence and impersonalism: the third stage is relativism. Not only is man reduced to an incident in the unfolding of an impersonal reality, but, even while he lives and moves, he is denied the power to know the truth of things. This, or something like it, is the ultimate outcome of the critical movement within philosophy itself, and of the psychological and sociological study of thought which has gone on in the last hundred years. To Christians, it appears as the greatest error and the greatest evil of the three, since it robs Christianity itself of the right to reply to the other two. It might be possible to answer the doctrine of immanence by urging that there are other sources of knowledge, not recognized by our contemporaries, which are open to us; but then the relativist comes in and says that we only talk like that because we are of a certain psychological constitution, or because we stand in certain social relationships, and at once all discussion is stifled. It is characteristic of our time that this shift of perspective has taken place, and that Christianity is now regarded very widely, not as a contention to be faced and met, but as a phenomenon to be accounted for; not as a possible contribution to truth, but as an episode in the history of human imagination. This is the unspoken assumption of most of our non-Christian contemporaries, and finds open expression in two of the most challenging writers of the nineteenth century: Marx and Nietzsche. Marx takes all speculative thought, all mythology and all religion, as a symptom of social *malaise*. He tells us what particular type of *malaise* gave rise to the Christian myth, and what type of social revolution will finally make it unnecessary. Nietzsche, very different from him in points of detail, agrees with him in seeing Christianity as a symptom of social conflict, and specifically as a protest movement on the part of the dispossessed. But he goes on to tell us that, under the impact of modern science, all the guiding lights of past religion and philosophy have gone out, that God is dead and man is alone in the world, and that he must set to work to create for himself such truths and such values as will serve his will to power. The whole atmosphere of the discussion is thus anthropocentric and voluntaristic. Religion, like philosophy, is a human activity and is to be judged by the extent to which it satisfies human purposes; and, in the future, we must boldly set aside the Christian myth and the ethic associated with it, and refashion our lives on a more forceful pattern.

It is certainly no use trying to answer relativism by logical sleights. To argue, as some do, that a consistent relativism must assert its own relativity, and that true scepticism must be sceptical of itself, is neat and easy but off the point. For what we are dealing with is, not a contention which might be answered by a counter-contention, but a deep-seated attitude of the will, a despair, or at least a shifting of the focus of hope; an abandonment of intellectual aims and standards which have been determinative for our culture since the time of Thales, a redefinition of truth in terms no longer of *adaequatio intellectus cum re*, but of *ordinatio intellectus ad voluntatem*. The word is no longer "the case is thus, and thus I therefore believe", but "it is of use to society that the case should be taken to be thus, and thus I therefore take it". *Hoc volo, sic jubeo, sit pro ratione voluntas*. And this is not the motto of the un-principled man alone (it was always that), but the conclusion to which serious men are irresistibly led by the prevailing thought-processes of our time.

What is and what should be the Christian reaction to these developments?

There are those among us, pathetic remnants of the once triumphant liberal hosts, who still misconceive the trend of the time, and think they can march in step with modern thought to a positive and creative end. To these we can wish nothing better than an awakening in time, painful though it must be.

There are also those who see clearly whither the trend is leading, and whose reaction is one of firm resistance. The Catholic Church has taken up its position decisively against the modern movement, and, tracing its origins back along time as far as Descartes, has set itself to reaffirm the main lines of the scholastic synthesis which the seventeenth century began to break down. The human intellect apprehends the real essence of things; its commensurate object is created being as shown to us through the senses, and this it understands well enough to trace in it with rational certitude the creating and sustaining power of God. All the doubts which have latterly arisen are the result of a subjectivity which defaces not only modern philosophy, but also modern art and modern religion; and the critical movement in the last three centuries is dis-missed as the natural and regrettable outcome of this initial error. It is a strong position; for if the neo-scholastic sometimes seems to meet the modern challenge with mere assertions and dogmatic principles, he is able to urge that the abandonment of these principles, by the verdict of history itself, can end in nothing short of disintegration.

It is a strong position, but is it a Christian position? To this the answer, I believe, must be twofold. In face of error, as in face of evil, the Christian has a choice of two types of strategy. The first is that of firm resistance, stonewalling as it might be called, meeting every move of his opponent with a steady denial, and a steady reassertion of the principles to which he is himself committed. It is the technique of resistance as set forth in Ephesians 6: 10-17, and it fights the enemy to a standstill, but it does not destroy or convert him. The second type of strategy is that of comprehension, which enters into the mind of the enemy and transcends him from within. The Christian here is not the soldier of pure truth in conflict with the servant of the lie. He stands side by side with his opponent, sinner with sinner, under the judgment of God which condemns and transforms them both. He carries his opponent with him into the Presence, and shares with him both the inevitable death and the promised resurrection. To let down our barriers, to enter into the heart of the modern intellectual situation, to undergo in ourselves something of what the Christless world perpetually endures, and in the midst of the storm to invoke Him who commands the wind and the waves on behalf of those who do not know His name—this is not easy, but it is the only way of redemption. It is the way of the Cross, and, indeed, there is an intellectual as well as a moral and a spiritual Cross to be borne; but we cannot begin to bear it unless we have that in us which casts out fear.

Why, in fact, should Christians fear in the presence of the crisis in philosophy? Only if they have reason to think that the crisis can touch their own faith: and this it can do only if their faith is somehow dependent on philosophy. Here, then, we reach the kernel of the question. So long as Christians retain the view, characteristic of Thomism but not confined to it, that Christian truth rests at least in part upon foundations of metaphysical reasoning, so long they will be disturbed by every change of metaphysical fashion. So long as the philosophical reasons which are sometimes urged in defence of Christian theism are treated as if they were the real reasons upon which Christian theism itself is based, so long their Christianity can be threatened by counter-reasons from the same philosophical source. While this is so, there is no escape for the Christian but to try to freeze philosophy at the stage in its development which was most congenial to Christian interests, and to treat all tendencies on its part to develop in other directions as aberrations which are to be exposed and denounced. It is a denial of the Christian doctrine of history, but it is in line with other forms of the same denial which are to be met with around us to-day. The Christian mind as a whole has never made up its accounts with the Renaissance and all that has followed from it, and its penalty is that it can no longer speak to our age where it is.

Mi frater, mi frater, excoquenda est ista tua philosophia. These words were spoken to a man in search of faith. But surely if any man ever believed, Wesley believed at that time and had believed for years. Had he not given proofs of it in action, in his austerities in Oxford and his adventurous voyage to America? Yes, he had done this; and now he was in search of faith, and doubting his right even to preach or teach until he had it. Was then his previous faith a thing of naught? In his own judgment, at any rate, both then and later, it had missed the central point of Christianity. For he had accepted a tradition in which he had been brought up, he had devoted himself most earnestly to the pursuit of that aim which the tradition set before him, and was firmly persuaded that the whole tradition was well grounded and should command the assent of any reasonable man. But now this is not enough. Now Jacob is caught in a personal encounter, and must wrestle through the night until the day breaks and he wins a blessing. Is not all this a parable for us? God is not known so long as we believe what we are told about Him, nor even when we buttress this belief with reasons drawn from the wisdom of the ancient world. God is known only when He is met, and that is when He comes to meet us, whether it be in the assembly of His people, or in the reading or hearing of His Word, or in the midst of the storm where He appears and with His simple I AM casts out fear. The intuition of primitive man is not wholly astray, after all. In the tumult of the impersonal forces of nature and of history the personal presence of Christ is found. And Christian faith is simply the recognition of this encounter when it occurs.

This has nothing to do with philosophical speculation, and though the Faith may make use of words and thoughts coined by philosophers, it cannot be undermined by their enquiries. For the divine encounter is life, and life is the master of thought. It is here as it is with our knowledge of one another and our recognition of one another as persons. This is not a theory, but it stands in judgment on all theories, and any philosophy which cannot do justice to it is thereby condemned. Even so, the presence of God in His world and in the events of history stands in judgment on any philosophy which can find no room for it. What hinders men from recognizing this presence is not the cogent reasoning of the philosophers, but something more intimate and more deeply rooted in the mind: inhibitions, unwillingnesses, prejudices, all of which in the end reduce to a fear of committing oneself to the unknown and incalculable. Likewise what opens the mind to the recognition of His presence is not the work of philosophical analysis or constructive argument, but a readiness to lower one's barriers and throw oneself open to a transforming influence. The man who passes from the one state to the other, from unfaith to faith, is neither convinced nor persuaded. He is converted. And that to which he is converted is not a new theory replacing what he previously held, but moving within the same thought-frame as before, not a better version of the attempt which he was already making to bring the world of experience into order through a particular set of categories. It is itself a rival and a more comprehensive thought-frame, a new set of categories and a new principle of synthesis, which can include and transcend the ordinary one and set it in a new light.

If faith does not rest on philosophy, neither does theology. If Aristotle was right from his own point of view and in his own age when he made *theologia* the flower and crown of metaphysical science, his conclusions are no rule for Christians, who have acquiesced too long in his version of the case. The speculative theology of the pagan sage is one thing, and the revealed theology of the Christian is another. Our theology has its own foundation in God's own acts and words, and is not only not dependent on philosophy, but actually capable of putting the whole philosophic enterprise in its place among the activities of man, fallen and redeemed. And therefore theology can dare calmly to confront the negative results to which recent philosophy has been led, accepting them for what they are worth, in their own place, as a judgment on what had gone before, and asking what the hand of God is doing in and through all this. What is the Word of the Lord through Locke, Hume, and Kant, through Marx, Nietzsche, and Dilthey?

We have come to the end of a chapter in world history. The new methods of enquiry which revolutionized our ideas of the physical world in the seventeenth century have now revolutionized our ways of living and our attitudes to one another. We are living in the midst of one of the two or three great world revolutions which have decided for long ages the destinies of man. As once the whole face of life was changed by the discovery of the arts of agriculture, pottery, weaving, and the consequent growth of settled urban life; as the intellectual stature of man was increased once for all by the rise in the first millennium before Christ of the great philosophies and the philosophically inspired world religions; so to-day the world and man are both being radically changed by the new scientific knowledge and its application. Philosophy as we have known it belongs to the period of world history which is going out. The question before us is, what form the activity of the philosophical mind will take in the new world that is to come. It will certainly be changed, and its relations with Christianity will be changed also; and thus not only the world, but the Church and its relations with the world, must come under judgment and reformation. Of those relations the Christian attitude to philosophy is a part, and it is in that context that the question must be seen.

We need not, in this wide perspective, be surprised if the trend of philosophy to-day is towards a radical critique of itself and its own past tradition. It is no wonder if the powers which we once thought we had are now found to have been in part illusory. The great constructive systems of philosophy served in their time as a propaedeutic to the Faith not only for individuals, but for a whole civilization and a whole continent. That was their historic mission, and now it is discharged they must submit to a searching judgment. It is written: "When the perfect is come, the partial shall be done away."

> *Advenit veritas, umbra praeteriit,*
> *Post noctem claritas diei subiit . . .*
> *Cum Christo prodeunt cuncta de latebris,*
> *Nec locum deserit lux tanta tenebris.*

But if the world has now to be weaned from its attachment to its old idols, what of the Church, which made a pact with these idols? It, too, must be purged and set free from what would now hinder its growth in the truth. The movement of criticism, which is breaking up the philosophical tradition from within, is destined also to break up the hold of that tradition on the Christian mind. The providential significance of the modern crisis, both in philosophy as such and in its relations with Christianity, is thus that both the world and especially the Church are being summoned to submit to a purgation of the intellect, to enter the active night of the spirit. And, if so, then the tendency of many Christian apologists to reassert dogmatically the foundations of ancient metaphysics, and to talk rudely about modern writers whom they have not always understood, may be no more than the natural reluctance of human nature to enter upon the darkness of that night.

VII

THE STATE AND DIVINE LAW

By W. A. WHITEHOUSE, M.A., B.LITT.

THE authority of the State, the measurement of its justice, and its relation to the Kingdom of God, are problems raised in a more acute form to-day than perhaps at any time since the New Testament was written. That the State is an instrument of God is a doctrine derived from Scripture, and maintained in some form by all Christian thinking. But can this doctrine be affirmed with regard to contemporary States, in a form which takes account of their alienation from Christian faith and morality? The most disreputable, perhaps, of Europe's rulers, declares that in his country "people get that social justice which is compatible with order and a sense of authority. We are right, and God is with us. God will not allow barbarism and brutality to rule over us." Elsewhere, men are confronted with the theory and reality of completely secular States, which make far-reaching demands on their members in virtue of an "authority" consisting chiefly in the State's possession of supreme means of power, physical and psychological. Again, in liberal-democratic countries, the idea that "authority, not wisdom, makes the law" has gained much ground. Politicians may still speak of justice, tolerance, freedom, etc., as a basis for politics; the coercion of the individual by the State may be well concealed in such countries; but the majority of democratic politicians grow increasingly unsure of their ground when they seek to base action on principle rather than on expediency. If the State is a divine instrument, it must be subject in some clear way to the divine law, and it is hard to see how this may be held as true in the case of any of the contemporary States.

Subjection to the Law of God implies, in Christian thinking, moral responsibility. No mechanical operation of a "law" in nature or history does justice to the relation which must exist between God and His instrument the State. Again, this subjection implies that no State can ever be regarded as an arbitrary expression of the will of the people or of their governors. They may have conceived it as such, but in fact they lack the power to preside over its office and destiny. Its history will bear evidence of the divine law, and at every point a moral obligation is conveyed, whether or not it be acknow-ledged. Again, Christians cannot but suppose that this moral obligation will issue in a service rendered by the State within the Kingdom of God proclaimed and established by Jesus Christ. We have to enquire about the existence of such a divine law, and the nature of the State's subjection to it.

It is possible to raise this question at a level where all men are equally concerned, and in terms to which all men can subscribe. Christians and non-Christians alike are concerned to re-establish the authority of law in political theory and practice, and to safeguard the morality of the State's use of power. The norm by which State activity is to be directed, on this level of thinking, has to do with such matters as the preservation and nurture of human life, the rights of man, the development of his nature and personality, the reformation and defence of the secular structure within which he lives, and the establishment of a just and lasting peace. But discussion on this level presupposes a prior understanding of the place which the State has in the purpose of God for the present world, upon which Christians are not agreed. It will be necessary therefore to look at a group of questions which lie properly within the Christian theological sphere, in order to conceive a context for the supposed subjection of the State to divine law. This matter has been brought to the fore by Karl Barth and Alfred de Quervain, both of whom speak in a new way of the political order as an order for the service of God. The question they raise is implied in the Declaration of Barmen, the standard adopted by the German Confessional Church in 1934: "We reject the false doctrine that there are spheres of life in which we belong, not to Jesus Christ, but to other masters; realms where we do not need to be justified and sanctified by Him." The primary reference of this to the National Socialists' claims for German blood and soil and for their own party-State, is clear and straightforward. But it may well have a bearing on the political doctrine of the seventeenth-century Reformers, and that of developed Lutheranism and Calvinism, as well as on the Roman Catholic theory focused in the doctrine of Natural Law. It may well appear that the authority of "God" upon which the justice of the State is deemed to rest in all these theologies, is something other than the authority of Jesus Christ made known by the Gospel. If so, recent developments in New Testament exegesis (particularly of such passages as Colossians 2: 15 and Ephesians I: 9, 10) provide a ground from which to criticize traditional thinking of all kinds, and from which the context with which we are now concerned may be seen more clearly. In passing, it may be noted that the encyclical *Quas Primas* issued by Pope Pius XI on the occasion of the establishment of a new Church festival, the Feast of Christ the King, bears evidence of a like Christocentric thinking, though the Pope's development of the thesis is unlikely to commend itself to Protestant thinkers.

I. The State and the Kingdom of God

Both Roman and Protestant[1] thought about politics rest traditionally on an implicit denial that the revealed Kingdom of God has any *direct* bearing on the theory and practice of politics. The reality of the State, and its office, derive from an order prior to the redeeming work of Christ. From the Catholic standpoint, "St. Thomas bases political philosophy on natural reason and natural law, not on revelation and supernatural theology. . . . Thus it remains that the rights and duties of citizens are not changed in substance through supernatural theology or baptism. The natural motives are strengthened through supernatural motives, but they are not superseded by the latter. The divine law that issues from grace does not abolish human law that issues from natural reason. In its field the State and the citizen have therefore a genuine though not

[1] cf. Brunner, *The Divine Imperative*, p. 443 and Note 7 on p. 680. "The Reformers have no Christian philosophy of the State, any more than they recognize a divine *jus naturale*. They take seriously the statement that the State is a secular order *alongside* of the Church, and it is at this point that virtually the idea of the State based on Christian ideas is abandoned." I dissent from Brunner's analysis on p. 443, mainly because of his peculiarly Continental Protestant use of the concept "nature"

absolute autonomy."[1] Revealed truth has its part to play in strengthening natural motives and purifying them. Further, "it was a salutary step forward to human freedom when St. Thomas and the doctors of Late Scholasticism based their political philosophy upon reason and natural law, and took away from the State its sacred theological majesty, its divinity with which paganism had consecrated it."[2] Nevertheless, it should be clear that this procedure rests on a theory of law and of the State which is ultimately theological. It is all very well to say that "political institutions are not to be judged by the theological errors which ideologically called them into existence, but by their conformity to natural law", but this presupposes acceptance of the Roman Church's conception of the dealings of God with the world of men. It arises from an ideology which may well be based on theological error. What is the context of this doctrine of the natural law?

God created men, and the world in which He set them, with the purpose of establishing the human race in supernatural communion with Himself. The Kingdom of God which accomplishes this purpose is realized in the relation between Christ and His believing people; that is to say, in the Church. The powers of Christ in His kingdom are communicated to His people, and though not realized in their fullness in any individual, they are completely deployed in the total hierarchically ordered life of the Church. The Kingdom may therefore be identified with the Church of Jesus Christ, made visible through the ages in the Roman communion under the headship of the Pope.

The bearing of these powers on politics is to reinforce in man the active principle of natural community, which can be apprehended by the intellect, and affirmed in moral freedom in particular concrete acts which establish a State, whose end is "right order", expressed, preserved, and developed by the proper functions of the State in the community. This political life gives to all men the possibility of self-realization of their social nature, towards an end of natural self-sufficiency. The supernatural end of communion with God is attained by grace in the Church. The Kingdom of God in the Church embraces

[1] Rommen, *The State in Catholic Thought*, p. 112   [2] *op. cit.*, p. 116

that whole life of man, and it is from the Church that the believer learns true political life, in terms of "Natural Law". He learns that politics is concerned only with the natural life of man. As a political creature, made for community with his fellows, he affirms the State as an ordinance of God which guarantees the public order, and expresses the inner moral necessity that the lives of individuals be organized in community. He learns also to require of the State, to which he gives political allegiance, that it acknowledge the supreme status of the Church as above all other communities. For the rest, the action of the State must be based on the structure of creatures as natural beings. This structure, both in its present actuality and in its perfection, so it is assumed, may be perceived by the human mind; then the will is laid under obligation to realize in free human acts the greatest possible perfection of man's nature in the natural and moral cosmos. In actual fact, human sin prevents true perception, much more true implementation of the Natural Law; and the Kingdom of God, revealed by His grace in Jesus Christ, alone is able to deal with this weakness of moral nature. But man's life in the State, even when he is aided by grace, is still strictly natural. The State is necessary to the natural life of men who are also in the Church, and may indeed operate so as to drive others to grace, but of itself it is unaffected by the order of redemption.

The State, and the Natural Law to which it is in principle subject, have here only a preliminary connection with the kingdom of God established in Christ. His Incarnation and Atoning Work have no bearing on the law by which the State's operation is to be measured. The subjection of all things to Christ (including the State), acknowledged in *Quas Primas*, is expressed in the "spiritual authority" which the State should accord to the Church.

Protestant Church thinking has not, of course, assigned such a positive and optimistic significance to what is achieved in the sphere of nature. The foundation of Church thinking about that State is to be found only in the order of creation, and the judgment of the divine law upon it, which are revealed in Scripture. The consequent tendency is to leave the State alone in the sphere of the lost world, requiring from it only such freedom for the Church as will promote the proclamation of the Gospel. If the ruler of a territory be a personal believer, he is expected to take responsibility in the community life of the redeemed Church—special responsibility indeed, in virtue of the office he holds in the State. In this case, the way is open for conceiving his political office by means of a theocratic model based on Scripture. If he is not a believer, he is summoned to hear the Gospel and believe, and to live by the forgiveness of sins rather than by self-justification. Again, there are Scriptural models from which to interpret his office. If he denies to the Church its freedom, he is still to be honoured, by the Church enduring suffering at his hands as did Christ at the hands of Pilate. In either case, his political duty is discharged on the basis of an authority delegated to the State by God in His Wrath, for the restraint of sin, the preservation of order, and (in His secret mercy) for a paedogogical function of bringing men to repentance and so to Christ. The law which he serves, and by which citizens may measure their own loyalty, is the divine positive law revealed in such portions of Scripture as are deemed to be Law rather than Gospel.

Though the conception is of Church and State standing alongside each other in a given territory pursuing diverse interests, rather than of the Church presiding spiritually over States; and though, further, the temper differs from Roman thought, in that the Christian, knowing that he cannot "Christianize" this piece of fallen nature, accepts passively whatever it cares to do in its own sphere; Lutheranism has not departed radically from Catholicism on the one point that the Kingdom of God in Christ is realized only in the Church, and so the State and the divine law to which it is subject have only a preliminary connection with that kingdom. The State is conceived as operating in a realm which is not yet subject to Christ—nor, perhaps, ever can be. Christ's rule, as Bultmann has reaffirmed in his recent commentary on the Fourth Gospel, must not be called political, since Law and Gospel, State and Church, differ fundamentally in their character. The two spheres must be co-ordinated, with very little interpenetration. In Romanism, on the other hand, the State is conceived as spiritually subordinated to the Church. But, in both cases, there is a radical separation of the Kingdom of God from the earthly kingdom.

Calvinism differs from Lutheranism in declining to separate Law and Gospel so sharply. The Law is a *demand* for the life which is *offered* by the Gospel. Calvin himself was aware that the Lord is the king of kings, and in his hand are the hearts of kings and the revolutions of kingdoms. "No government can be happily constituted unless its first object be the promotion of piety, and all laws are preposterous which neglect the claims of God, and merely provide for the interests of men." Quoting Jeremiah 22: 3, he says that: "*Righteousness* means the care, patronage, defence, vindication, and liberation of the innocent; *judgment* imports the repression of the audacity, the coercion of the violence, and the punishment of the crimes of the impious."[1] We may unfortunately agree with him that the "nature of this argument seems to have no connection with the spiritual doctrine of faith" discussed in the rest of the *Institutes*. He sees the promulgation of the Law as an eternal act of sovereign divine grace, but this is a "general" grace, not integrally bound up with the Person and Work of Jesus Christ. As a result, he was able to conceive (in opposition to Lutheran thinking) that the natural order may, in virtue of "the rule of the saints", become the scene of Christ's open rule —a conception which proved illusory both in Geneva and in seventeenth-century England. In other contexts he conceives of Church and State existing side by side, each in its own right, each serving the purpose of God. The political order is affected by the Person and Work of Jesus Christ only in so far as State and Church must come to terms with each other. Outside that direct contact—admittedly a nerve-centre for the whole matter —the State's responsibility to God is interpreted by elements in religious thinking other than the Kingdom of God established in Jesus Christ. The statesman is a minister of God, subject to His law, and the Church's demand for freedom for its own life and witness serves to conform the statesman's actions to this law of God and guide him in the promotion of piety and justice. But only by virtue of saving faith and membership of the Church can he ever be said to be a servant of Jesus Christ.

[1] *Inst.*, IV, 20, 91

The English Calvinists had a clear conception of the world as a twofold system: a scheme of nature, to which man, as man, belonged; and a scheme of grace to which the elect belonged.

Although, as has just been implied, Calvin seems to have no clear relation in mind between the Kingdom of God in Christ, and the political order, it has recently been suggested[1] that he is feeling after a more Christocentric account of the situation than has yet appeared. He believes that the atoning work and heavenly reign of Christ have positive consequences for the State and its office. He is ready, for that reason, to speak of a political justice derived from natural law, which must be sought and upheld in the name of Jesus Christ. It is worth noting in passing that he held an Occamist view of law, as deriving from will rather than from reason. He would not, therefore, with St. Thomas Aquinas, have articulated a doctrine of natural law in terms of access to the divine Reason by means other than the mediation of Jesus Christ. In certain passages he seems to conceive the State as owing its present reality, office, and authority, by reference to the kingly office of the exalted Redeemer. Article 50 of the *Heidelberg Catechism* speaks of the ascended Christ as "the Head through whom the Father rules *all things*" in distinction from His Lordship over the Church.

In line with this, Barth and de Quervain[2] have raised the fundamental question whether there is a theological basis for the State which is related directly to the grace of God in Jesus Christ. The State, in this Age of Grace between the times of Christ's ascension and His return in glory, has an office and operation different from those attributed to it by reference only to the Creator-God, or to the God who restrains sin in His Wrath. It does, of course, preserve the purpose of creation, and its office is still to restrain sin. In this it is a sign that the old world has not yet passed away. But, with the New Testament writers for whom the issue was raised as acutely as it is to-day, we may also regard the State as a worldly power which has been "spoiled" (Colossians 2: 15), and brought into

---

[1] W. Niesel, *Die Theologie Calvins*

[2] Barth, in *Church and State*, and in *The Knowledge of God and the Service of God*, as well as in his wartime letters to Czechoslovakia, France, and Great Britain. Alfred de Quervain in his recently published *Kirche, Volk, und Staat*, which is Volume II of his *Ethik*

the service of Christ and the Gospel. From the New Testament, especially from the part played by Pilate in the Passion Story, it is plain that the State survives by virtue of the forgiveness of God. In its own way, and amongst all men, it serves the Lord whom believers love as their Saviour. What is achieved by the State is not inferior or subordinate to what is achieved in the Church. Its service is a service of Christ to which believers and unbelievers are alike summoned, and which both are capable of rendering by virtue of His saving work. Its significance lies in the fact that the whole creation now looks forward to the final triumph of God's Kingdom in a new *political* order, to which the nations will bring their glory. In spite of sin, and in face of unbelief, the State exists in the service of Christ, to promote the extension of the Kingdom of God, by securing the preaching of the Gospel, and by the achievement of neighbourly love. The statesman and citizen, whether they are believers or not, should discharge their political obligations in a way which promotes the cause of Christ in realms which are not the Church, nor are subject (even "spiritually") to the Church.

In deriving from this theology a conception of divine law to which the statesman *as such* is obliged, we may however learn from Romanism not to confuse theology with political philosophy, but rather to derive a true philosophy, intelligible apart from faith, from the scrutiny of reality in the light of theological perspectives. Further, traditional thinking of all varieties serves to remind us that there is a proper independence of civil government from ecclesiastical—as opposed to divine —jurisdiction. To say that the law which establishes the State in truth and justice and imparts to it its rightful authority is integrally related to the Person and Work of Jesus Christ, is not to imply that the true end of the State will be achieved when it has become the Church, or the instrument of the Church. On the contrary, the Church acknowledges a work of Christ in the political realm other than His work in her own life. State and Church exist therefore, side by side, inter-related and interpenetrating; but in the action of both there is positive *Christian* significance. In particular, the State, as English-speaking Christians have sensed obscurely for a century or more, is positively connected with the order of redemption.

II. *The State as a Moral Institution*

The State has been defined as a nation organized for action under legal rules. Gladstone spoke of it as "the self-governing energy of a nation, made objective." Brunner says "the State is a definite ordering of the nation. . . . It confronts not only every individual, but also the collective body of its 'subjects' as an independent entity, and yet it is never anything else than the will and thought of these very people poured into this mould."[1] We are dealing therefore with a factor in human life whereby authority is exercised over individuals for the sake of public order and for the achievement of a common good in a national community. To it is committed the monopoly of supreme power, and its exercise of moral suasion is backed by coercive power. What is the derivation and meaning of this factor in human life, and how can moral responsibility enter into the situation if it be conceived as subject to divine law?

The doctrine that "the powers that be are ordained of God" is susceptible of a simple, primitive, and perhaps inherently pagan interpretation, in terms of divine right. Authority is delegated to the rulers of a nation by that nation's divine Lord. They are invested with a theological majesty, and, in virtue of their office, they share the mind of God. The word translated "ordained" means, however, "appointed", "arranged", "set, in a certain station". All that is affirmed therefore is that States exist by the will and purpose of God. The rulers have no inherent divinity, and they hold office in virtue of their ability to share the mind of God.

If, on the basis of Ephesians 1: 9, 10, it is said that in faith we know the secret divine purpose for the State, it remains for us to explicate this theological knowledge in terms derived from a rational examination of the State. First, we ask whether, and to what extent, this purpose can be discerned in the natural roots from which the State grows. Rational examination at once compels recognition of the ambiguous character of these natural roots. The reality of political government in national communities has a long history, explicable in terms of economic, psychological, and strategic necessity. Positivists are content

---

[1] Brunner, *The Divine Imperative*, p. 441

to find here the clue to the mystery, and to explain the State in terms of a balance achieved between mankind and natural forces, and between various opposing human interests. On the other hand, it is clear that rational human judgment has played a great part in creating a given State. Citizens have affirmed its authority on the basis of a rational or intuitive recognition of its nature and purpose. This affirmation has been an act of moral quality, not to be confused with the operation of mystical and mechanical efficient causes such as produce order in physical and biological nature.

At this point, something must be said about the persisting consequences of the Fall of Man for this expression of corporate life. There is a tendency in Protestant thought to explain the whole existence of the State as a consequence of sin. The attempt is sometimes made to fix on some feature, such as the State's use of coercive force, as *the* place where manifestly it is irremediably involved in the Fall. To criticize this approach is not to deny that the problem of power is an urgent one—the more urgent now that modern weapons and techniques have given to the omnicompetent State a complete insurance against the threat of the citizens to rise in their might against tyranny.

In my judgment, there is no feature of the State's existence which can be wholly identified as deriving from the Fall. The effect of the Fall is subtle and all-pervasive. The authority of the State is exercised by men who are sinners. Its inherited conception of its task, the circumstances within which that task is discharged, its tradition, and its resources of power, are all the product of sinful men acting in a sinful world. This appears in the constant danger that any State will act in complete self-sufficiency and irresponsibility. It appears also in the domination of all States by vested interests, which work against such political reformation as may be necessary for the right response to a given situation. At any time, the perception of the State's duty will be imperfect because of the self-justifying blindness of sinful men—believers and unbelievers alike. The situation in which it must act is one created by past sin, and statesman and citizen alike are bound by this chain of guilt to choose the lesser of two evils. The State is therefore

o

always liable to become the instrument of human selfishness and not the instrument of the justice of God.

The same things, however, can be said about the life of the Church. The life and office of the Church are to be distinguished from those of the State, because the life of the Church, rooted in the objective atonement wrought in Christ, is a life of liberation from sin. The Church *is* the Church by virtue of its humble *acceptance* of divine forgiveness. The State operates among all men, where forgiveness of sin is not accepted in the absence of universal saving faith. The State, therefore, if it be a minister of Jesus Christ, operates in a context where His redeeming love has not free course. But that is not to say, either that its operation is derived not directly from His redeeming love but from some neutral "nature", or that the context of this operation is wholly coloured by human sin and divine Wrath.

This being so, are we justified in saying that the State, with its ambiguous derivation and its sin-corrupted life, is derived from the will and purpose of God and in particular from the act by which His purpose is accomplished in face of human sin, that is to say, from the Work of Jesus Christ? Are we justified in regarding the State as a *responsible* form of human life, answering to the creative and now redemptive demand of God? If so, this demand is conveyed in the secular realities (or natural roots) from which the State and its work arise, and in the rational apprehensions from which men create the State in acts of free moral responsibility. This, I think, is what the Gospel bids us believe. Any State is a sinful organism, acting in a sinful situation, but by virtue of Christ's redeeming work and the subjection of the State to Him, it is possible for that State so to act that, in the name of Jesus Christ, its action may be upheld as right. When it does so, that action will also be affirmed as reasonable and just by all men of good will and right reason. This is the truth behind the classical doctrine of Natural Law.

In this context, very different from his own, we may find verbal agreement with the statement of a Roman Catholic philosopher of great wisdom: "The universe is order, cosmos not chaos. It is the eternal law, the divine reason, which has instituted this order. Since free rational beings can intellectually grasp this eternal law, and through it the will of the divine legislator, for them this order becomes the natural law. In the light of reason, man recognizes the order as one that ought to be realized by himself. . . . Non-intellectual creatures follow their nature blindly without moral responsibility. Intellectual free beings ought to realize their free, rational, and social nature in freedom. In the last resort, accordingly, there is a coincidence of the laws of biological life and the natural law."[1] The order instituted by God *in His act which redeems the fallen creature* may be recognized in the light of reason as the order that ought to be realized by man's free acts of moral responsibility. Thus, through the existence of the State and the discharging of political responsibilities, all men enjoy a measure of the freedom which Christ has bought for mankind. The State, in its own limited way, serves the purpose of the Kingdom of God established in Jesus Christ.

This thesis calls for a re-examination of the process whereby the duty of the State may be discerned. For this, man needs the light of a rationality set free by the work of Christ to function reliably within the secular realm. Such discernment will not come without reference to the Gospel, but that is not to say that it can come only to believers. True, only the believer can see the State's task within the perspectives of God's purpose revealed in the Gospel; and these he will see only in so far as he is willing to expose himself to the technical-ities of political life wherein the demand of God is conveyed. These realities in themselves have an autonomy relative to the Gospel revelation, and the help which experts can give in exhibiting them is independent of the experts' faith or unbelief. But when they are seen within the perspective of the Gospel, the believer is able to speak of them rationally; and there seems no reason why this rational illumination, once it is established, should not be a light in which unbelievers also may see and take action.

It may be questioned whether this task of "theonomic thinking"—as it has been called[2]—has been faithfully dis-charged in the past. In Roman thinking, it seems that fallen

[1] Rommen, *op. cit.*, p. 181
[2] A. R. Vidler and W. A. Whitehouse, *Natural Law; a Christian Reconsideration*

nature is too readily accepted as bearing upon itself the will of the divine legislator. In Protestant thinking, the criterion for the divine purpose of the State is taken to be an account of divine positive law, derived from the Bible but not integrally related to the Gospel. Theonomic thinking implies, for those who are affected by it, a genuine sharing in the mind of God, and the possibility of a true response to His Will. This gives the ground for asserting that the State is a moral organism, and that there is such a thing as corporate conscience in a State. The nation is therefore responsible to God for what is done in its name. The State exists as a form of national life whereby certain corporate functions are responsibly discharged. As such, it is derived from the will and purpose of God, and plays its part in the Kingdom He has established in Jesus Christ.

III. *The Response of the State to Divine Law*

This fundamental thesis must be explicated in face of the questions disclosed in political philosophy. What is the conception of divine law, relevant for the politician as such, which arises within the world order which God has instituted by creation and redemption? If, for the State to discharge its office under Christ, it is not necessary to postulate saving faith in all men or even in its officers, there must be some relation between political activity and divine law which is significant for the politician as such. It was suggested in the last section that man is given access to the mind and purpose of God in so far as he apprehends this order by living through historical situations, reflecting upon them in theonomic thinking, and acting in the light of such thinking with moral responsibility.

The divine purpose is effected in the development of history, however incomplete may be the apprehension thus made possible, or however inadequate the response to it. Pilate's betrayal of his office served in its own way towards the establishment of the Kingdom of God in Jesus Christ. The persecution of the Church by a pagan or apostate State serves in its own way to promote the Kingdom of God; and the Church, by its willingness to suffer in such circumstances, respects the divine ordination of the State. Nevertheless, the purpose of divine law is realized only partially, the possibilities of a given historical situation have an incomplete fruition, where there is not true discernment of the divine law, and morally responsible affirmation of its demands by statesmen and citizens. Therefore, as Barth says, the Christian community should expect from the State such action as will promote the interests of Christ and His Kingdom.

The promotion of Christ's work by the State should, of course, be conceived in different terms from those which apply to the service of the Church. Here is the root of the distinction between Law and Love which has produced much confusion, especially perhaps among English-speaking Christians. Obedience to law, it is supposed, must be essentially self-regarding, and therefore must be in an entirely different order from the realm of love created by the Gospel. The action of love is free self-giving. But if the moral content of love be safeguarded, then love's purpose is partially effected in a situation where the free gift is unappreciated or rejected, by means of a demand for righteousness. Law may be described as love operating at a distance. Now in the political life of mankind, God's gift of Himself in Jesus Christ is not, in general, appreciated; occasionally it is openly rejected. This is not true of the Church, whose office among believers is, therefore, quite different from the office of the State among all men. God's dealings with men through the State are works of law, but what is effected thereby is a measure, permitted by the situation, of His purpose of Love; and that purpose is "to sum up all things in Christ" (Ephesians 1: 10).

The divine law by which the action of the State is measured, is communicated to it in a threefold contact with the life and thought of the Church.

First, the State must deal with the Church as with an earthly institution, existing within its territory in a certain form. It is a means of grace to the State that the Church seeks from it peace and freedom for its own witness to the Gospel by word and life. Jeremiah exhorted his captive brethren to "seek the peace of the city whither ye are carried away captive, for in the peace thereof ye shall have peace." In claiming freedom for its preaching and its own form of life, the Church contributes towards the peace and well-being of the State. It is no part of this essay to elaborate the duties of the State to the Church, or the duties of Christians to the State, but two points may be noted here. First, if this claim for freedom is to be a means of grace to the State, the Church must take seriously the form of its own life. The contribution to political life in England made by the claims of the Reformed Churches for freedom for their peculiar form of church life is an illustration of what may happen. Secondly, the demand for political conditions wherein Churchmen can serve the State with Christian integrity, is itself a means of grace, provided that such men are concerned to make their demand felt either by criticism or revolt whenever conformity is impossible. Barth makes the interesting suggestion that the "good" referred to in Romans 13: 4 ("The ruler is the minister of God to thee for good"), is not some neutral "good" of nature, but rather the Christian "good" established by the Gospel in the lives of believers.

Secondly, the State has to reckon with the Church's proclamation of true religion. The responsibility of the State, if interpreted from the Ten Commandments, is not confined to the second table thereof. The Gospel proclaimed by the Church summons the State to free itself from paganism. The State cannot itself be the organ of true religion in the sense of faith in the Christian Gospel, but it may not commit itself to an official religion other than Christianity, if it is to serve its purpose in the world where the Father rules all things through the exalted Christ.

Thirdly, there are areas of political decision which are affected only indirectly (if at all) by these direct contacts with the institutional Church. Contact with the Gospel is implicitly achieved, however, in the practice of theonomic thinking, where such technical matters may be scrutinized in the light of divine law, reason being the guide acknowledged by believer and unbeliever alike—reason redeemed for its true purpose by the work of Christ.

Before introducing the characteristic features of the State's response to divine law, let me quote an excellent account of the place of law in the Bible:

God's lordship over the world and over the societies of men is

214

not left in Scripture as an abstract principle, but finds expression in concrete ordinances given for the regulating of man's relations with the material world, on the one hand, and with his fellow men on the other. . . . This law is not an Old Testament conception which is, as it were, a mere approximation or moderately successful guess at the requirements of God, which is outdated by the Gospel. On the contrary, it is the instrument of God's love which ever regulates the life of men as creatures in history, and which, while it is fulfilled by the Gospel, will never be superseded until the end of the world. . . . To take this Biblical category of law seriously would deliver a good deal of Christian thinking from the confusion in which at present it stands. For example, it is sometimes put forward as a matter of debate among Christians whether they are or are not justified in compromising the law of love for the sake of justice. If we lay hold on the Scriptural insistence that God's law is an instrument of His love, we shall be at home with the related idea that justice in the communities of men is the mode by which love becomes operative. The Bible is not at home with the question of compromise, because it does not deal in ideals or principles, but with the service of God in and through the concrete conditions of man's historical existence. The service of God is the love of man, and love of man in the large-scale life of society expresses itself in the struggle to establish and maintain justice with freedom on a basis of material security.[1]

What, then, may be said about State action in these areas of political decision not directly affected by the existence of the Church or by its characteristic life and concerns? Does consideration of the State's task yield the possibility of reference to the divine law through which all things are subject to Christ? It is perhaps foolish to risk making the broad general comments which alone are possible within the scope of this essay, but they may serve to indicate directions along which careful enquiry would be profitable.

The activity of the State is to create justice and to restrain evil. But this task it pursues for the sake of the citizens who, as neighbours, are bidden to love one another, and not in the interest of an absolute impersonal justice, or an indestructible world order. This service consists, it is true, in the establishment of an external order, but this order is not for the sake of the State's own prestige. In itself, it is not holy or good, nor has it any intrinsic worth. "Righteousness" has, in Scripture, a

[1] Alex Miller, in *The Presbyter*, June, 1944

soteriological reference. It is associated with the vindication of the poor and oppressed, and can never be dissociated from mercy and grace. To philosophize about the bestowal of righteousness upon creatures, we must begin from the revealed righteousness of God and not from a rationalization of human or natural justice. In every age, and in every society, some agreed conception of justice must be reached in political thinking before the society can live together in peace and blessing; nor can it be doubted that the history of political thought and action since the time of Christ bears marks of His lordship over earthly States. This is true of Marxist developments, as much as of the growth of Social Service States. These modern developments, like the earlier development of liberal-democratic political theory, are not "Christian"; indeed their effect may be to increase the temporary danger that the State will become an instrument of human selfishness rather than of divine justice; but their significance can be most clearly discerned in relation to the Gospel, and in their own way they bear testimony to its truth. Also they bear witness to an increasing apprehension of depths in the justice commanded by God which hitherto had not been plumbed. This apprehension is faulty, and the response may in practice be perverse.

Granted the primary point that State action should be for the sake of persons, and that its major concerns are to be understood in relation to the divinely instituted order of redemption, there are four spheres wherein moral responsibility may be clarified with reference to divine law.

(a) It is the task of the State to ensure the primacy of human law over its own ideas and interests: to establish the rule of law and the impartial administration of human justice (conceived with reference to humanity rather than to impersonal natural order), so that a measure of personal freedom and integrity is preserved for the individual and the social groups within the State.

(b) The State must also ensure the safety of the community from external enemies and from internal disintegration. A national government which does not treat its Home Office and its war potential with the utmost seriousness is not worthy of confidence. But its penal methods, and its practice of warfare, involve serious moral issues which need constant and careful scrutiny.

(c) The cultivation of mental and physical health, and of civil virtues, is again the responsibility of the State. The standards it accepts must be based on an understanding of humanity, must be appropriate to the best kind of civilization which man has achieved, and must be modified wherever possible and reasonable by distinctively Christian insights.

(d) It is the responsibility of the State to strive for a right solution of the economic problems which so intimately affect civilized living. Here, as in the other spheres, the subjection to divine law of State action in regard to Labour, Industry and Trade, Agriculture, Finance, etc., needs long and careful explication. Perhaps the most important aspect of the present political situation is the possibility of vastly increased control of man's environment and conduct through the resources of scientific thinking. Is it not perhaps true to suggest that this also should be understood with reference to the purpose of God established in Jesus Christ; His purpose, namely, to elicit from men a fully moral response, in political as well as individual life, to His saving righteousness.

LIST OF PRINCIPAL WORKS BY KARL BARTH

In German

SAFENWIL PERIOD

Suchet Gott, so werdet ihr leben (sermons by K. Barth and E. Thurneysen), 1917.
Der Roemerbrief, 1919.

GOETTINGEN PERIOD

Der Roemerbrief (2nd Ed.), 1922.
Das Wort Gottes und die Theologie, 1924.
Die Auferstehung der Toten, 1924.
Komm Schoepfer Geist, 1924.

MUENSTER PERIOD

Vom Christlichen Leben, 1926.
Erklaerung des Philipperbriefes, 1927.
Die Lehre vom Worte Gottes (Prolegomena zur christlichen Dogmatik), 1927.
Die Theologie und die Kirche, 1928.
Zur Lehre vom Heiligen Geist, 1930.

BONN PERIOD

Fides Quaerens Intellectum (Anselms Beweis der Existenz Gottes), 1931.
Die Kirchliche Dogmatik I 1, 1932.
Theologische Existenz Heute, 1933.
Nein: Antwort an E. Brunner, 1934.
Credo, 1935.

BASEL PERIOD

Die grosse Barmherzigkeit (sermons by K. Barth and E. Thurneysen), 1935.
Rechtfertigung und Recht, 1938.
Die Kirchliche Dogmatik I 2, 1938.
Die Kirchliche Dogmatik II 1, 1940
Die Kirchliche Dogmatik II 2, 1942.
Die Kirche und die politische Frage von heute, 1939.

Translated into English

The Word of God and the Word of Man, by Douglas Horton. Pilgrim Press.

The Christian Life, by J. Strathearn McNab. S.C.M. Press.

Questions to Christendom. Lutterworth Press.

The Resurrection of the Dead, by H. J. Stenning. Hodder and Stoughton.

Come Holy Spirit (Barth and Thurneysen). Round Table Press, New York.

God in Action. Round Table Press.

The Epistle to the Romans, by Edwyn C. Hoskyns. Oxford University Press.

The Doctrine of the Word of God (*Dog.*, I, 1) by G. T. Thomson. T. and T. Clark.

God's Search for Man. Round Table Press.

Theological Existence To-day, by R. Birch Hoyle.

Credo, by J. Strathearn McNab. Hodder and Stoughton.

Church and State, by G. Ronald Rowe. S.C.M. Press.

The Knowledge of God and the Service of God (Gifford Lectures), by J. L. M. Haire and Ian Henderson. Hodder and Stoughton.

Trouble and Promise in the Struggle of the Church in Germany. Oxford University Press.

The Church and the Political Problem of Our Day. Hodder and Stoughton.

A Letter to Great Britain from Switzerland. Sheldon Press.